An Architectural Journey in Japan

AN ARCHITECTURAL JOURNEY
IN JAPAN

By J. M. Richards

THE ARCHITECTURAL PRESS · LONDON

Printed in Great Britain by THE SHENVAL PRESS, London, Hertford and Harlow

CONTENTS

FOREWORD

SO MUCH INTERESTING BUILDING—and indeed important building in relation to world-wide developments in architecture—is now going forward in Japan that long and expert studies could well be devoted to different aspects of it. This volume does not claim to fill this role, nor to be in any way a comprehensive account of modern Japanese architecture. It is simply an illustrated day-to-day narrative of a visit I paid to Japan last year at the invitation of the Foreign Ministry. The purpose of the visit was to look at buildings and meet Japanese architects, and so the narrative naturally gives first attention to architecture and architectural trends and practices, but—especially in a land so unlike one's own—one cannot look at buildings independently of the setting they inhabit and the life they serve. This is also, therefore, a traveller's impressions of the modern Japanese scene.

The narrative is interrupted by short essays on aspects of Japanese architecture that seemed to me to require describing in some detail, and by photographs and plans of the new buildings I thought the most interesting, but I must emphasize that the whole book is the product of a two-and-a-half weeks visit— far too short a time for an authoritative survey. These are simply my personal impressions. No opinions are given that were not formed on the spot and (except for some of the pictures that accompany the biographical notes at the end) no buildings are illustrated that I did not see.

J. M. R.

The greater part of this book first appeared as a special number of The Architectural Review, *and so my first acknowledgments and thanks must go to that magazine. Grateful acknowledgments are also due to the Japanese Foreign Ministry whose hospitable invitation was the occasion of my visit to Japan, to Mr S. Shigihara of the Foreign Ministry's staff in Tokyo who acted as guide and interpreter, to Professors Kenzo Tange and Takamasa*

Yoshizaka who, on behalf of the Japanese Architects' Association, helped the Foreign Ministry to plan my itinerary, to Professor Tange again for the trouble he took and the time he spent helping me to spend my own time wisely and enjoyably, to the many other Japanese architects who showed me buildings and patiently answered questions and to the magazine Shinkenchiku *for help over photographs. The photographers whose pictures I have used are individually acknowledged at the end of the book.*

FIRST DAY

THE TEDIOUS JOURNEY TO LONDON AIRPORT can appropriately be occupied, as the car ploughs its way among the diesel-fumes along the somewhat improved highway carved through suburbia, in trying to eliminate from one's mind, in order to arrive in Japan as free as possible from preconceptions, the ready-made picture, sub-consciously pieced together since childhood, of the country and its people that everyone carries about with him.

A picture of a people 'clever as a pack of monkeys', able to imitate anything, inscrutable beneath their courteous manners; of gardens full of dwarf trees, stones, ponds and little bridges; of cherry-blossom, paper lanterns and distant views of Mount Fuji; of the modular planning of traditional houses and ceremonial tea-drinking seated on cushions on the floor. A picture of cinema films full of subtle imagery and violence; of over-decorated vases, the hideousness of *cloisonné*-ware, verandahed tea-houses imitated in Bournemouth; as contrast, the exquisite design of cutlery and little boxes seen at international exhibitions. A picture of a small-statured people (except when they are wrestlers), frequently spectacled, emotional, friendly but implacable as enemies; of stylized women (Utamaro) with high-piled hair stuck with wooden pins, warriors in chain armour, waterfalls (as in Hokusai and Hiroshige prints) and coolies in the rain wearing wide-brimmed straw hats; of bicycles and cameras cheaply and expertly manufactured. A picture of remote wars fought from battleships with rows of upright funnels; more recently, of jungle warfare: the horrors endured by prisoners and world guilt about Hiroshima; of modern architecture, strongly influenced by Le Corbusier, vigorously rectilinear like timber turned to concrete; of teeming cities where the mysterious East mingles untidily with the industrialized West.

The effort is made, and the car pushes its way past the huddle of shacks along the airport boundary and through the tunnel to the long-haul passenger building: a very respectable new building, cleanly and boldly finished inside, with nothing to affront the most design-conscious visitor except the stock of souvenirs in the gift-shop. The usual long delay before departure, with nothing to do but drink un-wanted cups of coffee and stare out of the windows, brooding on the seemingly insoluble problem of the clutter that occupies the spaces between buildings.

Take-off at last: the aircraft a DC8c, its spacious interior only marred by opulent but inappropriate brocade upholstery. Stewardesses (now that air travel is accepted as a matter of routine by everyone, the term air-hostess can surely be discarded) in Japanese dress—kimono and obi; but how difficult for an Englishman (inherited memory of generations of light opera?) to regard this particular foreign costume as anything but fancy dress; no other costume—certainly not the Indian sari—is so difficult as the Japanese to accept objectively away from its native land. The process of ridding one's mind of preconceptions is clearly not so easy as was thought.

No such problem over the next Japanese custom encountered: a basket brought round containing damp towels, steaming hot and rolled into little sausages, for wiping one's hands and face—the prelude, which one never ceased to welcome later, of every Japanese meal and a service provided in bars, inns and railway-trains. Next, though the flight to Paris is only thirty-five minutes, a snack on a tray: strawberries and cream, sweet biscuits, coffee or tea—the first of those oddly com-posed meals characteristic of long-distance air-travel, served at strange intervals and in a strange order, that do so much to upset one's already confused conception of the passing of time.

Paris soon—a very brief stop; then off again to Copenhagen—a strangely domesti-cated city to be the taking-off point for the North Pole. Another meal on a tray, this time a multi-course lunch; chop-sticks provided but not obligatory; Japanese dishes if preferred. The route passes over Cologne and Hamburg, but nothing visible except a layer of cloud above which the high-flying jet aircraft cruises in bright sunshine.

Copenhagen in an hour and a half: down through the cloud; glimpses of ice (or could it be detergent?) floating in the dark waters of the sound; hazy roofs and towers and masts of shipping; touch down in a snowstorm. But the stop at Copen-hagen a pleasure because of its charming airport buildings: discreet outside, airy and unusually agreeable in, high-roofed and with something of the character of the turbine-hall of a power-station, with overhead walkways supported on gantry-like exposed steel frames; austere but good in colour and scale.

Away again after refuelling in less than an hour, up through the low cloud on the long flight, straight over the Pole, to Anchorage in Alaska. It's now just on 2 p.m. Flight time is eight hours, so we shall arrive about 10, but as Anchorage time is eleven hours behind Copenhagen time we shall in fact arrive at 11 in the morning—three hours before we left, another complication of jet air-travel (and a tip to all such travellers: don't continually alter your watch as the official time changes; leave it as it was or you'll have no means of knowing when you need sleep or a meal).

Up the coast of Sweden. Holes in the clouds show blue-grey sea but the shoreline and the many water-courses frozen; a snow-covered landscape varied by dark patches of forest, soon becoming hillier and less forested, the only snow-free places the rocky sides of mountains. Next across Norway from Oslo to Trondheim, but cloud again obscuring the land below. Then along the coast to Bodo; after that, straight for the Pole, passing over Spitzbergen on the way.

4.14 p.m.: a present of an egg-timer—its significance unexplained, but it is one of the traditions of long-distance air-travel in the first class that souvenirs and comforts should be continually distributed in the intervals between the distribution of drinks, lavish (though progressively indefinable) meals and, in the case of Japanese aircraft, steaming rolled-up towels. In such air-travel, if nowadays in travel of no other kind, pampering the traveller is still thought proper and so is the creation of an enjoyable atmosphere of conspicuous waste.

By Spitzbergen the sky has cleared—brilliant weather now; snowfields far beneath, interrupted by angular mountains; then soon the Arctic sea, solidly frozen, crossed by zigzag channels differentially coloured as with washes of Payne's grey. But soon those blue-grey tones disappear—the water, one supposes, is now more deeply frozen—and then the creeks or channels disappear in their turn, giving way to the featureless flatness of the Polar plain.

Broad daylight still. When we had climbed above the clouds on leaving Copenhagen the sun was low in the sky but shining strongly into the port-side windows, and there it has remained since we are flying as fast as the earth is turning. On over the Pole itself. The sun stands still, and time (and indeed the vibrating aircraft) seems also to stand still while underneath unrolls, like a sugar-coated abstract painting, the flat dreamy Polar landscape, white and grey-white, covered with a network of fine ridges, touched by the evening light and emphasized by sharply cast shadows—the whole scene sparkling in the sun.

Seven hours from Copenhagen and a change of landscape: the mountains of Alaska, which come into view as a voice on the loudspeaker announces the expected arrival at Anchorage at 10 p.m. (11 a.m. local time); it is snowing hard there, says the voice, and the ground temperature is 30 below freezing.

Dramatically mountainous country now, tree-clad with curly rivers and pear-shaped lakes; the whole land glazed with ice. On the right, Mt. McKinley, over 20,000 feet, the highest in North America, its snowy pyramidal peaks reaching above the layer of cloud that now appears below us, like a cluster of islands in a woolly sea. Down into cloud out of the still bright sun, circling over frozen inlets, low cliffs, fir forest; no sign of life until the markings of a runway in the snow and a barely visible huddle of huts.

The cutting edge of the icy wind as one walks from the warm aircraft to the group of huts constituting Anchorage airport; then the overheated interior— suddenly very American: juke-boxes and slot-machines; tourist advertisements for the 49th State; ugly paintwork; shoe-shine seats elevated like thrones; tawdry local souvenirs and jumbo postcards. And then, just as one is beginning to reflect on the tastelessness of the casual Americanized scene, a sight of some local inhabitants—airport workers, perhaps, or mechanics or truck-drivers from the nearby town—exemplifying the characteristic dandyism of American working clothes: in this case high boots, fur caps, waterproof jerkins, worn with a becoming negligence.

Out again into the blizzard for the last leg of the trip. Men standing on the wings of the aircraft brushing off the snow. Take-off 12.40 p.m. local time; estimated flight time to Tokyo seven and a quarter hours. Out of the clouds into bright sunshine, but the clouds thinning soon: frost-bound inlets, snowfields, sunlit mountains. Across the mountains in brilliantly clear weather and out into the frozen Bering Sea. Then cloud below again, obscuring further view.

We are now losing time instead of gaining it. Tokyo time is five hours ahead of Anchorage, so we shall get there soon after 3 p.m. Having gained so much we are still in the day we started, but soon we cross the International Date Line and suddenly it is the same time next day, as we drum away over the North Pacific, visible now through breaks in the clouds, a deep grey-blue with fragments of broken ice.

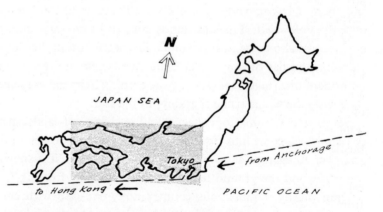

Map showing the four main islands of which Japan is composed, with Tokyo half-way along the Pacific coast of Honshu, the biggest island. The rectangle encloses the area of the more detailed map on page 42.

SECOND DAY

THE LIMITLESS BLUE OF THE PACIFIC—Coleridge's 'wrinkled sea', though it is a puzzle how he knew about this, never having been up in an aeroplane. In our cosily furnished cabin, hurtling through the upper air at 540 m.p.h., preparations for still another meal. Which meal, it remains to discover. By London (and therefore by one's stomach's) time it is 1.30 in the morning, much too early for breakfast; at Anchorage, which we have just left, it is already past lunch-time; by Tokyo time it is only 10 a.m. The meal turns out to be an elaborately planned dinner, but most passengers are by now too bemused by hour upon hour of unnatural daylight and too unsettled by changing pressures, temperatures and meal-times—as well as already too lavishly fed—to want to do more than nibble here and there and drink perhaps another glass of the frequently offered health-preserving champagne.

Over it one drowses and dreams, trying to read but unable to concentrate. Then, 2.10 p.m., Tokyo time, the first sight of Japan—the eastern coast of the main island of Honshu: shallow bays outlined by sandy beaches, wooded country beyond, a little snow on distant mountain-tops. Circling to land at Tokyo airport: glimpses of shipping, clusters of cylindrical petrol-tanks, the paraphernalia of a busy harbour. The airport itself—under reconstruction as airports always seem to be—the usual bustle and scurry on disembarking, then the long car-ride to the centre of the city.

The route from any airport to the city it serves tends to show the city's worst aspect (even visitors to delectable Paris experience disillusionment on the way in from Le Bourget), and Tokyo is no exception. Factories and shacks and a quite terrifying wirescape; a widish street thronged with noisy traffic and lined with a disorderly array of makeshift-looking two-storey buildings—workshops, dwelling-houses, open-fronted shops—largely timber-built, grey and dust-covered in the chilly sunshine of an early spring afternoon. Winter is the dry season in Japan and this one has been drier than usual.

The shed-like buildings interrupted by the carved brown gateways of Buddhist temples; also, strangely enough, by the high protective netting of golf-practice schools, for a craze for golf is just now sweeping Japan. Soon larger, more sophisticated buildings, but no more sign of formality or arrangement—the little timber

*Frank Lloyd Wright's
Imperial Hotel, Tokyo:
the main entrance front
seen from across the pool
that occupies the centre
of the forecourt and,
lower picture, a close-up
inside the porch,
showing the textures in
brick and stone.*

houses still scattered among them. At last, after many stops and starts in ever denser traffic, block on block of big city buildings, some crowned in distant views by strange lattice-steel towers, and, facing a wide main street, crouching at the back of its drive-in forecourt, the squat brown frontage of the Imperial Hotel.

The Imperial Hotel, Tokyo, Frank Lloyd Wright, completed 1922, one of the famous monuments of the early days of modern architecture (and threatened, like so many of them, with demolition), is made of the same material inside and out: yellow-brown brick and a strange, pitted, tufa-like stone. The outside is very little changed until you go round to the back and find the hideous, modernistic annexe that has recently been built on. Inside much has been altered (and the big banqueting room, bombed in the war, was rebuilt by the US Army in a style only vaguely resembling Wright's original), but the entrance and main lobby retain their basic, and very impressive, spatial arrangement: a broad low-ceilinged lower vestibule—a slight slope to its floor the only relic of the celebrated earthquake— leading to a high galleried foyer with garden courts beyond: effective and agreeable if you can manage not to scrape your elbows on the detail.

The bedrooms pleasantly old-fashioned; deep mosaic-surfaced baths; lifts called 'Fuji'; the intriguing discovery that light-switches in Japan are turned up for on and down for off—other reversals of English custom revealed themselves later: when beckoning with his hand a Japanese turns the fingers down, not up; he cuts wood by pulling the saw towards him, the teeth being set the other way; direction arrows, for whatever purpose, have one barb instead of two, thus:

But not much time now for observing local differences—or for that matter for unpacking; in half an hour there is a drinks party, to be followed by supper, given by the members of council of the Japanese Architects' Association. Called for by Kenzo Tange, professor at Tokyo University, designer of many remarkable buildings (of which more later) and author of a widely noticed new plan for Tokyo;

The brutal and characterless annexe which has been built onto the back of the Imperial Hotel.

15

mentor of the more intelligent young architects; quiet spoken, as are all Japanese, with an amused but watchful look and an incisive mind. Japanese architects are refreshingly free from the arrogance architects often display in the West.

What seems a long drive in the dusk along a bewildering sequence of contrasting streets—big city boulevards off which lead narrow lanes, sometimes steep and twisting, all teeming with people and noisy vehicles—the traffic in Tokyo seems nearer than in any other city to the stage where it will simply seize up altogether. In spite of the area over which the city spreads, the space occupied by roads is relatively small;* and another difficulty is that one-way traffic systems cannot easily be adopted because no street has a parallel one a practicable distance away. The underground railway is equally congested. A special body of men called 'pushers' is, it seems, employed on the platforms to cram the last passengers into the carriages so that the doors can close and the trains move off.

No street looks complete—half is old, half new—and modern commercial buildings alternate with groups of battered timber houses. Tokyo, more than any city imaginable, is an agglomeration of tiny villages, and village life goes on unchanged in the back land behind even the most central modern blocks. Neon lights reaching up into the sky give some coherence in the gathering darkness to the chaotic urban scene.

Arrival at the Architects' Association party and a great feeling of relief when confronted by the group of welcoming faces: they are all different. Was it only a legend learnt in childhood that to a Westerner all Oriental faces look the same—or was this only supposed to apply to the Chinese? Anyway the fear, created by this legend, of the social embarrassment that might be caused by not being able to distinguish whom one had met before and whom one had not, is now allayed: Japanese architects, at least, are as different from one another, even to the Western eye, as any readers of this narrative.

Ten or a dozen are present, among them Kunio Maekawa, this year's president of the Association and, along with Tange, the outstanding member of the fairly small group of sophisticated modern architects, Kenzo Ichiura, a specialist in landscape, Takamasa Yoshizaka, the shock-haired professor at Waseda University, Junzo Yoshimura, Yoshiro Taniguchi, Kisaburo Itoh, belonging to a somewhat older generation than the others (who are in age mostly well below fifty), Ryuichi Hamaguchi, a youngish architectural critic.

Talk at first on many architectural topics, but over drinks and then over supper it gradually settles down to a subject that seems particularly to be exercising the minds of the Japanese architects at this moment: that of the organization of the

* 9.2 per cent of the total, which can be compared with 23 per cent in London, 25 per cent in Paris, 35 per cent in New York and 43 per cent in Washington.

profession, the proper qualifications of the architect and his relationship to engineers, contractors and the like—a subject of course that the Japanese are not alone in worrying about but, judging from the information acquired on this occasion and later, their professional problems are more serious than most.

The Organization of the Profession

A Government licence is required to practise architecture. It is obtained after passing an examination controlled by the Ministry of Construction, and every building project must be in charge of a Government-licensed architect except for the traditional type of small house, if the floor area is not more than 100 square metres, which can be put up without supervision by a builder—in fact, a carpenter, since small houses are almost invariably of timber.

This sounds like a satisfactory enough system, but the first problem arises from the low standard of the qualifying examination, which is largely technical in its scope. Of the 30,000 Government-licensed architects in Japan, a great many are more what we might call building engineers or technicians.

These and the other less well qualified members of the profession constitute a kind of second class of architects, who have not taken a university course and passed the national examination, but have had six years' experience and have passed a local examination. But they too, it must be made clear, count as architects and can take charge of buildings.

The Japanese Architects' Association (*Nihon Kenchikka Kyokai*)—in certain limited ways the equivalent of the RIBA*—demands a high qualification but has a membership of only 450. It is an autonomous body (reconstituted in 1956) with no statutory position, electing its own members on the basis of reputation and executed work, after they have been sponsored by two existing members, as in a club. There is also a society to which architectural technicians who have not the qualifications to claim membership of the Association belong —the *Kenchikushi-Kai*.

The Japanese Architects' Association thus constitutes an unofficial élite, composed almost wholly of architects in private practice, and it has had to withstand over a number of years the strong pressure of the contracting industry against the architects' professional independence. For the big contracting companies—and this is another of the problems the profession is faced with in Japan—have their own architectural departments, some of them on a considerable scale. In the five biggest companies,† which are powerful organizations concerned also with building-finance and investment in property and land, these departments each employ a hundred or more architects, and they are responsible for more than a third of the total building work in the country.

The architects so employed are not eligible for membership of the Architects' Association. This exclusiveness on the part of the Association obviously has it dangers, among them the danger of putting the private architect on a pedestal and cutting him off from contact with the most important bulk of building activity and the development opportunities and opportunities of widespread technical co-operation that go with it. But it is a stand that had to be taken; otherwise there was the probability, when construction grew to an enormous volume after the war, of the architectural profession being wholly absorbed by the building industry and design standards and standards of ser-

* It has its headquarters in Tokyo and branches, analogous to the RIBA Allied Societies, in Nagoya, Kyushu—the southern island—and Kansai (the name given to the central area of Japan containing the cities of Osaka and Kyoto).

† The Obayashi and Takenaka companies with headquarters in Osaka; the Taisei, Shimizu and Kashima companies in Tokyo.

vice to the public being overwhelmed by commercial expediency. The Government—that is, the Ministry of Construction—exercises no professional control over the mass of architects when once they have passed the qualifying examination, and only the Architects' Association sets standards of professional conduct and responsibility and forbids undercutting of fees and the like.

In spite of the smallness of its numbers and the relatively small size of its members' offices—the largest contains perhaps forty or fifty assistants, but most far fewer—the Association has considerable prestige, partly derived from the independence of outside pressures that it has struggled to preserve, partly, it must be said, to good relations with the upper levels of the social stratification that is still of some importance in Japan and partly to the fact that important civic and similar commissions have lately gone to its members as a result of intelligent patronage or their own success in architectural competitions—commissions which have brought its members prominently before the public eye.

The Association seems to be well aware of the dangers of isolation and—under Maekawa's presidency especially—has been actively concerned about modern trends in architectural organization and the need for the architect to keep pace with them. But the need is felt, in self protection, to go on putting independence first. One incidental effect of the, so to speak, alternative bodies of architects within the contracting industry is the temptation they offer to private architects to delegate to the contractors some of their responsibilities. The contractors with architectural offices of their own are also, of course, among those which, following the usual tendering system, execute the private architects' designs, and some of the latter have adopted the practice of handing over only sketch designs, allowing the working drawings to be made in the contractor's architectural office, but this is a practice generally frowned upon by the private architects.

The best of the big contracting firms achieve, it should be said, in some of their work, first-rate standards of design, especially in office and industrial buildings; they have learnt much, in design and technique, from America. The best work of the Takenaka and the Obayashi construction companies in particular is as good of its kind as that of all but a few of the private architects, though perhaps more dependent on accepted modes of modern styling—see some of the office buildings illustrated in this book. Lower down the scale such styling predominates. These offices are notably up to date and efficient, with branches in most big cities. Though they have the advantages of the accumulated experience of many similar jobs, they have not the incentive to undertake development or research work, which is chiefly done in the universities—see the section on *Architectural Education*.

Some experimental work seems, however, to be going forward within the industry on the subject of the greater industrialization of building components, but this suffers from not having the interest and support of the more aesthetically educated younger architects—the price, perhaps, that has to be paid for the Architects' Association's necessary policy of avoiding entanglement with the building industry. The whole process of industrial integration is, in any case, only beginning. It chiefly shows itself in research into methods of house building in concrete, the traditional timber having suddenly become expensive.

One other form of architectural office has still to be mentioned. There are several big design offices—again employing some hundreds of architects—which, though operating as self-contained organizations, are in fact dependents of some of the big industrial and commercial corporations which play an important part in Japanese life, extending their operations over many different fields—banking, import and export, investment, manufacturing and trading generally. The architectural offices of this type were mostly set up in the first place in order to provide these corporations with the architectural services they needed—to design branch banks, factories, stores, garages and the like. Thereafter they expanded to take on private commissions as well, so that they now continue, as it were, under their own impetus but still with the advantage of being regularly fed with commissions from the parent company, which still also maintains some financial control.

The most notable of these is the Nikken company, founded and controlled by Sumitomo, a vast organization including among its activities banking, insurance and mining and controlling important elements of the Japanese chemical, aluminium and metallurgical industries. The Nikken company has four divisions; architectural, electrical, general engineering and civil engineering. The Nikken architectural office has done some distinguished work, at least as good as the best that comes from the big contractors' architectural departments. Its head office is in Osaka. It has branches in Tokyo, Nagoya and Fukuoka and an organization somewhat resembling that of Skidmore, Owings and Merrill in America. The biggest industrial corporation of all—Mitsubishi—controls a similar office. Architects working in such an office, since they are not directly involved in the contracting industry, are not debarred from membership of the Architects' Association, and several of the chief designers in these offices have in fact been elected to it.

If the big contractors' architects are responsible for a little over a third of the building work in Japan and private architects a little under a third, the remaining third is done by Government departments or other official offices such as those of the prefectures or municipalities. A lot of this is routine work, somewhat uninspired, but better quality work is achieved, as elsewhere, when there is someone outstanding in charge of the department. A notable instance in Japan is the architectural department of the Ministry of Posts and Telegraphs which, under the leadership of Hideo Kosaka, has set a standard new to official architectural offices and has acquired such a reputation that Kosaka and his staff have been called in to design public buildings outside the post and telegraph field, as in the case of the Foreign Ministry building in Tokyo. Kosaka is the one official architect with the same standing and reputation in sophisticated circles as the senior members of the Architects' Association.

The fact that there are only a few first-class architects recognized as such outside the profession makes it difficult for young private architects to get work to do—even architectural competitions tend to be limited to invited entrants—and to start up on his own needs a bigger effort than elsewhere. It also needs capital, because there still survives a paternalist tradition whereby architects do not discharge staff when temporarily short of work. Such difficulties may, however, have the advantage of driving the enterprising young architects, however ambitious they may be to run their own practices, to get experience in the meantime in the big contractors' and similar offices, and some are doing so, impelled no doubt also by the greater opportunities offered there to get close to new industrial ideas and methods. Nevertheless the separate status of the private architect who belongs to the Association, with his professional and aesthetic conscience, and the unorganized remainder is still the dominating factor in Japanese architecture.

THIRD DAY

A MORNING SPENT ON A SERIES of courtesy calls: on the Foreign Ministry (formal conversation and polite exchanges with the vice-Minister, over little cups of scalding tea); on the Ministry of Education (ditto, ditto); on the British Ambassador. The Embassy, unmistakable, but not undignified, Ministry of Works neo-renaissance, built in 1925 and standing in a large compound which also contains the Chancellery and several commodious houses for senior Embassy staff. Between these calls a more extended view of central Tokyo: many new and still uncompleted city buildings, scattered rather than forming a compact built-up core, mostly commonplace in style such as might be found in Philadelphia, Birmingham or Sydney, of even height but given a certain strangeness by the miniature Eiffel towers—in fact radio transmission towers—and the advertisement-bearing superstructures that spring from many of their roofs. One not-so-miniature, but more slender, Eiffel tower closes many city vistas.

The central part of the vast sprawling city is prevented from being utterly formless by the presence, right in the middle, of the vast tree-planted grounds of the Imperial Palace, a private open space abruptly and picturesquely defined by a moat with huge sloping retaining walls on the inner side faced with uncoursed stone, giving the roads that surround it on the outer, public side an open boulevard character. There's a recurring demand that these Palace grounds should be made available for building, to ease congestion at the centre, but they don't seem to be taken seriously by the planning authorities—and rightly, since they provide a unique and invaluable breathing space. But a plan for taking traffic tunnels underneath them—one of several official measures for easing the flow of traffic—seems sensible, has been agreed to in theory but in practice is going forward all too slowly.

Government buildings as conservative and dull as they tend to be everywhere, the only exception being the Foreign Ministry, respectable though unexciting, designed by Hideo Kosaka, architect to the Ministry of Posts and Telegraphs, and the newly completed Diet Library, a four-storey building with a strong horizontal emphasis, a little confused in its detailed wall treatment, perhaps because, although

20

Tokyo street scene. With its advertising signboards displayed vertically to take Japanese writing and its profusion of wires and poles to carry them, it is typical of the main thoroughfares of this and most other cities.

it was the subject of an open competition in 1953—the first big competition staged after the war—the winning design, by M. Tanaka and M. Ohdaka, was taken out of their hands and executed by the Ministry of Construction.

The problem of finding one's way about Tokyo. Not only is the layout of streets without pattern or consistent direction; the streets have no names. Some main streets have the remains of numbered boards put up in desperation by the American occupying army, but these count for little. There are main districts with names that everybody knows, smaller districts or wards within them, and then even smaller

Diet Library, Tokyo, the outcome of an open competition.

local neighbourhoods based on the village structure, and the process of finding an address is one of tracking it down, narrowing the range of inquiry until you are near enough for anyone to tell you where it is to be found—a process which seems to work, but at the cost of long drawn out colloquies with taxi-drivers and by-standers.

The authorities are said to be planning a means of more systematically identifying streets; of what kind does not seem to be known. It may be—as some philosopher has already suggested—that the present situation does not represent so much the negation of method as a stage of development beyond mere arithmetical order towards some profounder kind of apprehension. We can only wait and see.

Wirescape everywhere; trees tightly wrapped in straw against the frost, and grass (except where diligently watered) a yellow brown—it will only become green as the summer goes by, summer being also the rainiest season. The quantities of people in the streets, but all purposefully moving along (in contrast to the equally crowded streets of Indian cities, where the people seem instead to be standing around waiting). Their courtesy: no one stares at foreigners, so that even the most self-conscious can feel at ease. People with white gauze surgical-type masks covering their mouths and noses and tied with tapes behind the ears—a widespread habit, presumably against Asian flu or perhaps simply the cold spring air, which doesn't seem to inhibit communication.

After lunch, to Maekawa's office, a long three-storey reinforced concrete building with open ground floor, glass-walled above, that he built for himself in the difficult years just after the war. It houses about forty assistants. More talk, over little cups of tea, about the state of architecture and the status of architects and then out in his car for a visit to some of his buildings.

First to a new range of buildings for Gakushuin University, an ancient establishment that in feudal days was a school for the sons of nobles, now one of the forty or fifty universities that Tokyo possesses. An exciting moment this: the first sight of an example of that new architecture in exposed concrete by means of which

Maekawa, Tange and one or two others have drawn the eyes of the West to what is going on in Japan. By no means a disappointment: the influence of Le Corbusier evident but fully assimilated; a pyramidal lecture hall in the centre of a courtyard formed by rectangular buildings of varying façade pattern but given coherence by their consistent scale and by the way the deep-set apertures emphasize the weight and solidity of concrete slab walling.

Next to Ueno Park, a public park in north-eastern Tokyo within which, standing close together, are two buildings of outstanding importance for modern Japanese architecture. The first of these is the Museum of Western Art, built in 1959 to house paintings and sculpture—mostly French—bequeathed by a collector, the late Kojiro Matsukata; the building designed by Le Corbusier and executed for him by a trio of Japanese architects—Maekawa, Yoshizaka and Junzo Sakakura, all three of whom had worked in Le Corbusier's office in Paris, Maekawa and Sakakura before the war, Yoshizaka after. The Master's visit to Japan in 1955 was, one gathers, very brief and, perhaps for this reason, the building has less impact than his great works, though one should remember that it is only part of a more ambitious, uncompleted project.

Outside it is disappointingly neat: a square mass raised on pilotis, the only elements with any plastic vigour being a couple of external stairs. Inside, the central hall, rising through three storeys, does show Le Corbusier's customary command of space, but his special interest was clearly the lighting of the exhibition galleries for which he devised a characteristically ingenious and original system, bringing the light down from a series of glazed roof-structures into narrow wells descending

Maekawa's office,
designed by himself.

into the gallery-space, from which it is taken downwards through horizontal grilles to illuminate the wall surfaces and the pictures on them, and at the same time outwards to throw light across to the opposite wall. It is a system which perversely, though its aim is the exact control of light and though it succeeds in introducing natural daylight into unexpected recesses of the interior, has proved exasperatingly inflexible in practice. The curators of the gallery find it difficult to provide any given group of pictures with the consistency and intensity of lighting they require.

Alongside the Museum—indeed towering somewhat over it—one of Maekawa's most important buildings, the Tokyo *kaikan* or festival hall, roughly the equivalent of London's Royal Festival Hall but containing a small as well as a large auditorium, the former at first floor level. The foyer of the main auditorium particularly well handled spatially; such of its walls as are not glazed consist of the rear walls of the hexagonal auditorium, sloping inwards and faced with pebbly textured pre-cast slabs—the same surface that is used on the outside of the pyramidal roof higher up. This use internally of materials that the Western eye would expect to find more often on the outsides of buildings is typical of modern Japanese civic buildings. It gives them vigour and masculinity as well as, sometimes, a degree of grimness. The inner walls of the main auditorium are decorated with somewhat aggressive cut-out shapes in wood; the small auditorium much more successfully with projecting squares of concrete looking as though they were the outcome of some natural cataclysm—what might be called a kind of *béton trouvé*.

The exterior shows Maekawa's talent for the expressive use of concrete, which

(*continued on page* 37)

In the Ginza area of Tokyo; note the characteristic advertising superstructures.

Gakushuin University, Tokyo

architect: Kunio Maekawa

These additions to one of Tokyo's many universities consist of four buildings—see air view on page 27: a four-storey building providing research accommodation for the staff of the departments of political science, economics and literature as well as a couple of lecture rooms, another four-storey building of science laboratories, a two-storey administration building and a pyramidal lecture hall seating 700. Above: the lecture hall and the paved and planted courtyard from beneath the research building. Right: the administration building with the research building on the left.

Gakushuin University, Tokyo

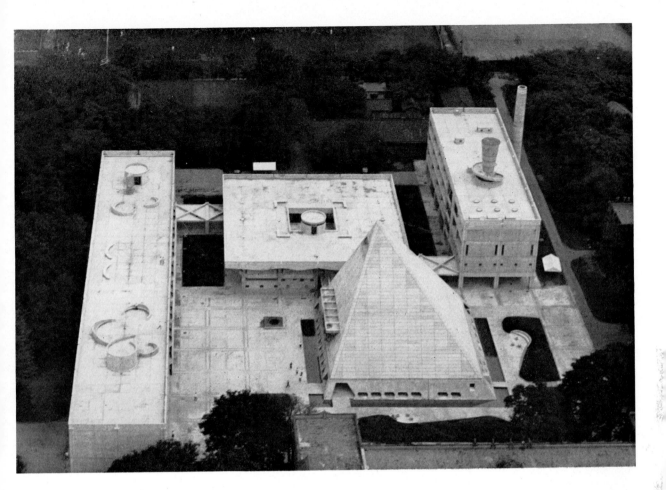

Air view of the four buildings. The pyramidal lecture hall is in a paved courtyard, enclosed by the other new buildings and some of the earlier buildings and entered underneath the research block (left in the photograph). This four-storey block is also shown in the photograph opposite. The pyramidal shape of the lecture hall prevents it cutting off too much light from the surrounding court and permits good lighting inside.

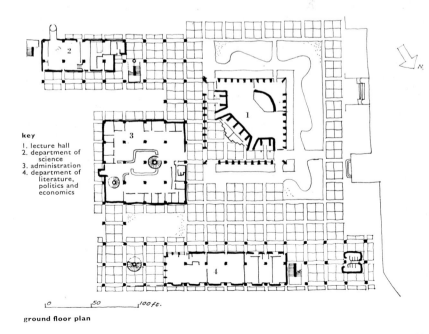

key
1. lecture hall
2. department of science
3. administration
4. department of literature, politics and economics

0   50   100 ft.

ground floor plan

27

Gakushuin University, Tokyo

Above left: the lecture hall, the administration building (on right) and the covered way connecting with the science block. Above right: the science block and the foot of the pyramidal lecture hall. Below left: the arcade formed by the frame structure of the lecture hall. Below right: its interior.

Museum of Western Art, Tokyo

architect: Le Corbusier

The ground-floor sculpture hall, rising through two storeys. The picture galleries are arranged round it on the first floor and reached by a ramp.

Museum of Western Art, Tokyo

Above: the south side, facing the paved forecourt and Maekawa's festival hall. The entrance is on the left, beneath the oversailing upper floor of the building. Below: the north side, with offices on the ground floor and picture galleries above.

Executed according to Le Corbusier's
design by three Japanese architects
(Maekawa, Sakakura and Yoshizaka)
who had worked in his office in Paris,
the museum, in Ueno Park, Tokyo,
stands behind a paved forecourt used
for the display of sculpture. The
paving extends beneath the building,
and the rest of the ground floor is
largely given up to the two-storey
sculpture hall shown on page 29, the
picture galleries being arranged
round its upper part. Top left:
glazed roof-structures that take light
down into the galleries (centre left).
Below: a staircase.

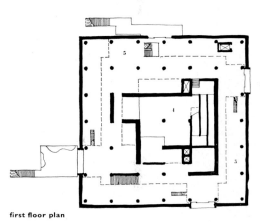

first floor plan

key

1. entrance hall
2. central sculpture
   hall
3. administration
4. upper part of
   central hall
5. galleries

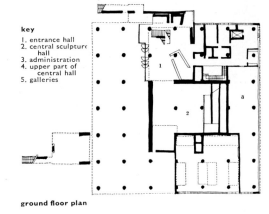

ground floor plan

Festival Hall, Tokyo

architect: Kunio Maekawa

Right: an air view of the festival hall. It contains a hexagonal main auditorium, designed for concerts and operas, a small auditorium on the first floor, square in plan but with circular seating, an exhibition gallery and a restaurant. The building was completed in 1960. On the facing page: the entrance front, showing the contour of the reinforced concrete terrace overhang, with the marks left by the timber shuttering.

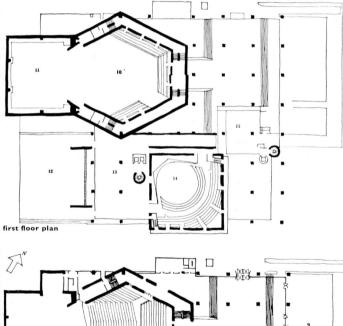

first floor plan

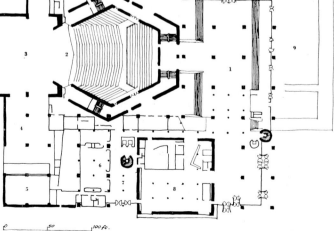

ground floor plan

0   50   100 ft.

key

1. foyers
2. main auditorium
3. stage
4. wing space beneath upper terrace
5. rehearsal room
6. administration
7. stage entrance
8. exhibition gallery
9. terrace
10. upper part of auditorium
11. stage tower
12. terrace
13. foyer
14. small auditorium
15. restaurant and bar

Festival Hall, Tokyo

The festival hall from the entrance forecourt (photograph taken from the roof of Le Corbusier's Museum of Western Art—see pages 29–31). This side of the building faces north-east. Facing page: the main double-height foyer showing the first-floor restaurant projecting into it. On the extreme left is the battered wall of the main auditorium.

Festival Hall, Tokyo

Above: the outside of the stage tower faced with pebble-surfaced concrete slabs. It has double walls for sound insulation owing to the nearness of a railway. Right: inside the small auditorium; the concrete wall-sculpture is by Masayuki Nagare.

the heaviness of the vertical members (required as a precaution against earthquakes) does not seem to spoil. The main cornice has the curved profile that Maekawa has used in several buildings—a profile functionally justified as a way of giving shelter from the rain without cutting off too much light, but in which some people have found a reminiscence of the characteristic shapes of traditional Japanese roof-structures.

In the evening, a stroll about the Ginza area of Tokyo with its main thoroughfare containing the big department stores. Brassy, uninhibited, commercially competitive, it looks its best at night when its vulgarities are subdued and illuminated advertisements, flaring up into the sky, take over. Tokyo does these advertisements and sky-signs splendidly—additionally attractive no doubt to the Westerner who cannot read what the writing says, but raising the whole question of how much they derive their vitality from their spontaneous, anarchical quality and whether this could ever survive an attempt to design them as a conscious form of civic decoration.

Almost alongside the Imperial Hotel, a barely completed new office building of unusual competence and sophistication, occupied jointly by the Tokyo telephone company and an electrical manufacturing company. Its quality is noteworthy because it came from the architectural office of one of the big contracting firms—the Obayashi Company—whose significant place in the modern Japanese architectural scene has already been noted.

Telephone building, Tokyo: an example of the sophisticated style of city architecture of which the best of the architects' departments run by the big contracting companies are capable, in this case the Obayashi Company.

37

FOURTH DAY

IN THE MORNING A CALL ON Yasugoro Yoshioka, the founder and proprietor (formerly also the editor) of Japan's largest architectural magazine, *Shinkenchiku*. He has more or less retired now and lives in a cosy villa with cage-birds chattering in a neatly tended back-garden: a venerable but bright-eyed and charming figure in heavy brown robes, tied with a black sash; slow conversation with the aid of an interpreter across the polished table over tea and sweetmeats speared on slivers of bamboo, in which the old man showed understanding and curiosity about happenings all over the world. Then to a lunch-party, arranged by *Shinkenchiku*, to meet a group of the younger architectural critics. A first experience of a Japanese style restaurant, approached like so many of them by a winding cobbled pathway from the street, flanked by evergreens and with water trickling among the cobbles; shoes off at the doorstep, then by narrow passages, wood-panelled with windows looking on to more evergreen shrubs that make gardens out of the minutest spaces, to the large high-ceilinged dining-room. In the centre a long, low table at which one sits on flat cushions cross-legged on the floor—racked soon, if one is a Westerner, by aching knee-joints and cramp in the thigh-muscles until one gives in and unobtrusively extends one's legs under the table.

Saké in little china cups, constantly replenished, and delicious Japanese food, the appeal of which subsequent experience confirms. It could not be more different from Chinese food, with which most Westerners are already familiar. Instead of being a mixture of ingredients, generally served wet, it is dry (except for the variety of soups), mostly baked or grilled, and each ingredient is separate and distinct. It is always beautifully garnished and served in an almost architectural pattern of dishes and bowls; colour and texture valued at the same time as flavour. Lobster, crab and a great variety of fish superlative, though the slices of tunny-fish or bream served raw take some getting used to. The foreigner soon learns to avoid small items like certain pickles that he finds too pungent for his Western palate, and a dried seaweed that appears at almost every meal. Meats and fish are dipped—a severe test of the skilful handling of chopsticks—into little bowls of soya sauce. The sign that the sequence of minuscule courses is coming to an end is the arrival of bowls of rice.

This is accompanied by soup and perhaps pickles; it may be followed by fruit, certainly by tea.

The fellow guests: half-a-dozen architectural critics. In Japan, strangely enough considering the relatively tentative stage that the organization of the profession has reached, the critic is an accepted if youthful figure, and the number of architectural magazines—running to nearly fifty, though some are small and infrequent—offers enough scope to allow criticism to be a full-time occupation, and the critics' opinions have some outside influence on the award of commissions.

Present: Hamaguchi (acquaintance already made), Tsutomu Ikota, Noboru Kawazoe, Charles S. Terry (*Shinkenchiku's* American translator who interprets) and other members of the magazine's staff. The critics are primarily critics of aesthetics, and are almost uncannily well informed about developments in all parts of the world; they are in contact with current interest in Gaudi and want to know what has become of Lubetkin, but though eager and intellectually mature, they appear to be far less interested in, for example, low-cost housing, the relation between architecture and town-planning and the industrial evolution of new building methods—a reflection, perhaps, of the cleavage between the leading private architects who are their heroes and mentors, and the busy, aesthetically anarchical commercial world where architecture and contracting are inseparably mingled, which the critics for the most part despise.

After lunch to the Olympic stadium in the Sendagaya district, an impressive enough but architecturally not very distinguished oval concrete arena designed in 1957 by the Ministry of Construction, where work is just beginning on the task of increasing its seating capacity from 55,000 to 85,000 in preparation for the Olympic Games to be held at Tokyo in 1964. With standing room the enlarged stadium will hold 100,000 people.

More evidence of the enthusiasm for golf that is sweeping Japan: it is Saturday afternoon, and along the forward edge of the upper tier of seats, 30 feet or more above the ground, is a row of young golfers, silent and as intent and self-sufficient as a row of anglers beside the Seine, indefatigably practising driving. Each stands on a square of coconut matting and has a crate beside him filled with dozens of golf balls. One by one he tees them up and drives them away into the open spaces of the arena, where the groundsmen go about their business of laying turf and repairing the surface of the running-track, disregarding the rain of golf balls but protecting their heads with portable wire shields like sections of a nursery fire-guard.

From the stadium to the Suidobashi *Noh-gakudo* (theatre) to see a *Noh* dance in progress. This is a formal, symbolic dance-sequence that has been performed in almost unchanged style since the fourteenth century, unintelligible to the foreigner —and, one suspects, to most Japanese—but the subject of a cult, like the cult of the ballet among the British, on the part of devotees who form themselves into clubs where they discuss and analyse the classical repertoire of *Noh* dances.

The theatre crowded with people of all ages, some quite poorly dressed, listening and watching with intense concentration or in a kind of hypnotic doze, some following the proceedings with the help of printed texts like concert-goers following music with a score. A square boarded stage with sloping roof, projecting into the auditorium and reached by a raised gangway running along one of the side walls. Dramatis personae: a girl dancer, brightly costumed, who glides, advancing and retreating with little steps, reinforcing her gliding movements with stiff gestures of arms or fan; a kind of chorus, lined up in two rows along the side of the stage, kneeling and seated, immobile except for occasional minor but significantly timed changes of position and the opening and shutting of fans, joining vocally with the wordless music; an orchestra of three or four—stringed instruments and drums, the latter beaten with the flat of the hand to the accompaniment of curious, abrupt hooting cries on different notes whose rhythms it takes a while to pick up.

The dance, which continues for many hours during which members of the audience come and go, is too archaic and formalized for the stranger to appreciate, but is elegant, mysterious and suddenly moving when the evident rapport is felt like an exchange of wireless signals between the dedicated actors and the devotees who are concentrating every faculty on their performances.

Straight from the *Noh* theatre to the main railway terminus to catch the night train for Hiroshima—a twelve-hour journey. Bustle and clamour; the station—halls, staircases and platforms—packed with people, but once on the train order, quiet and control. Well-appointed sleeping compartment (the ingenious space-saving design of all such places, in plan and in section, has its special appeal to the architectural eye) and a punctual departure; slippers, dressing-gown and tooth-brush provided. Dinner in the restaurant-car and a long walk back, staggering as the train sways round a curve, between the curtained bunks of the third-class sleepers through which limbs protrude and are withdrawn as the inhabitants acrobatically disrobe within. Early to bed as the train—there's nothing quite so foreign as the noises foreign railway trains make in the night—grunts and rumbles its way across the central plain of Japan.

FIFTH DAY

AFTER DRAWING THE BLINDS AT FIRST light to observe the unfamiliar country-side—rocky, forested hills and bright green valleys of patch-work cultivation—a call from a kindly conductor to explain that an early rise has become unnecessary because, owing to engineering works, the train is running a couple of hours late. Breakfast in the restaurant-car and eventual arrival at Hiroshima—in fact, two and a half hours late, to the great satisfaction of many of the passengers; for this is a limited express, for which a supplement has to be paid over and above the ordinary fare, and the rule is that if such a train is more than two hours late the supplement is refunded. Long queue at the station of passengers getting their money back.

By taxi through the streets of the reborn city, which now has a population of nearly half a million. The main streets, at least, have been rebuilt to a reasonable width, but scrappily and with that brittle, makeshift character that seems normal even in the centres of Japanese cities; the architecture miscellaneous and un-distinguished.

Large but miscellaneous buildings—all of course new—in Hiroshima's main street.

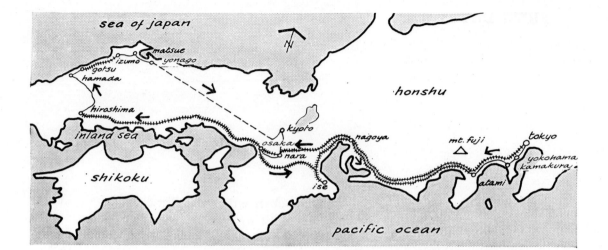

Map of the central part of Japan (see general map on page 12). It shows the principal places referred to in this book and the itinerary followed during the journey on which the text is based—from Tokyo to Hiroshima, across the mountains to the northern coast, south-east to Kyoto and Osaka and then back to Tokyo by way of Ise and Nagoya. The mode of travel is indicated by a solid line for road, a crossed line for railway and a dotted line for air.

An excursion by car to Miyajima, a famous Shinto shrine. Hiroshima is built on a delta where the Ota River flows into the Inland Sea. The road crosses several branches of the river, now very dry, revealing wide gravelly beds, and then runs close to the seashore past straggling fishing villages—the Hiroshima region is one of the main centres of the oyster fishing industry. Piles of oyster shells alongside the road; some to be ground up for fertilizer, others—already strung together on strings like calcined Christmas decorations—to be suspended in the sea for the young oysters to attach themselves to.

Outside Hiroshima a point where old timber houses can be seen leaning at odd angles; it's a mile and a half from the point where the atomic bomb dropped, far enough for the houses to survive, though pushed sideways by the blast. On to Miyajima, an offshore island reached by ferry, the location of the shrine, otherwise hardly visible among thickly planted woods, marked by the huge red Torii gate (the structure, shaped like the Greek letter π, that forms the entrance to all Shinto shrines) standing romantically in the sea.

The shrine itself a complex of timber buildings, gaily and newly painted in red-lead colour, some built over the water, some climbing the hill towards a crowning pagoda, the whole approached from the landing-stage by a long double line of tawdry souvenir shops. Crowded with visitors—the Japanese are indefatigable patrons of their own tourist sights—all with cameras. Incidentally the visitor to Japan need never feel self-conscious or marked out as a tourist because of going about the streets with a camera; the Japanese carry them everywhere, but they seem to use them chiefly for photographing each other.

Back to Hiroshima and, after lunch, to the Memorial Park, where the one large building that in part survived the atomic bomb—a hall for industrial exhibitions—has been preserved as a grim memento, its dome a skeleton open to the sky, and where also stands Tange's grey concrete memorial hall. This is a long exhibition gallery, walled with vertical louvres, raised on pilotis; a simple impressive conception, though roughly finished and not well maintained. Inside, a permanent exhibition—models, charts, relics and horrifying close-up photographs—of the

Hiroshima street scene; comparison with the pictures on pages 21 and 101 shows how closely Japanese cities are coming to resemble each other.

*Miyajima: buildings of
the Shinto Shrine.*

atomic destruction. One visited it from a sense of duty and shrank away from it at
every step, almost as much appalled by the groups of chattering school-children
who stared apparently unmoved by the most macabre exhibits. But it may be that
insensitiveness is not the explanation; simply that they had lived with the idea of
such horrors all their lives.

In front of the memorial hall: the 'peace bridge' across one of the arms of the
river, with parapet designed—fantastically but very successfully—by the sculptor
(and garden and furniture designer) Isamu Noguchi. Then to the only other new
building of interest in Hiroshima (apart from the prefectural offices, which are dull
but workmanlike): the Roman Catholic church by Togo Murano, an older pioneer
of modern Japanese architecture; a building with an exposed concrete frame and
infill walls of pinkish brick, influenced perhaps by Perret. It has a detached tower
with a baptistry at its foot, oddly Byzantine in style.

Tange's memorial hall, incidentally, is rather important in the history of modern
Japanese architecture, being (with the possible exception of Antonin Raymond's
Reader's Digest office in Tokyo, of which more later) the first of the modern
buildings in exposed reinforced concrete which have drawn the eyes of the rest of
the world towards Japan. There are in fact four pioneer buildings from which the
most interesting modern architectural developments in Japan all stem: Tange's
memorial hall at Hiroshima (1950); Sakakura's art gallery at Kamakura (1952);
Maekawa's concert hall and library at Yokohama (1954) and Tange's city hall at
Tokyo (1955). The last two were the outcome of limited competitions, with about
six architects, including Maekawa, Tange and Sakakura, invited to take part in
each case.

(continued on page 49)

44

*At Miyajima, an island in the Inland Sea, near Hiroshima, with a
celebrated Shinto shrine: the 55-foot high red-painted* torii *gate standing
in the sea. The photograph is taken from the shrine and has the mainland
in the background.*

At Hiroshima. Upper picture: the Roman Catholic church; architect, Togo Murano. Lower picture: the Peace Bridge near the memorial hall with sculptured parapet by Isamu Noguchi.

On this and the next page: the four pioneer buildings by Japanese
architects which constitute the classics of the early years of modern
architecture. Above: Tange's memorial hall at Hiroshima, 1950 (see also
page 49). Below left: Sakakura's art gallery at Kamakura, near
Yokohama, 1952. Below right: Maekawa's concert-hall and library at
Yokohama, 1954 (the photograph shows the end of the concert-hall wing
from the rear courtyard).

The City Hall at Tokyo, designed by Kenzo Tange in 1955.

48

Tange's memorial hall at Hiroshima, taken from the end of the Peace Bridge—see also page 47.

Then to the hotel—a *ryokan* or Japanese-style inn. In the big cities and tourist resorts there are of course many Western-style (or more precisely, American-style) hotels, but the Japanese hotel determines the way of life of the normal traveller and gives the visitor a taste of the many still formalized aspects of Japanese life. For this reason, and because architecturally it is related to the long-standing and still lively tradition of the Japanese house, the hotel, its layout, conduct and customs, are worth some detailed attention.

The Japanese Hotel

It generally exposes only blank walls to the street, or a high garden fence interrupted by an arched opening. It is turned inwards on itself. It is seldom more than one storey high, though there may be minor changes of level within.

The deeply bowing proprietor greets the customer in the doorway. Bowing behind him are members of his staff, including the maid who is assigned to look after the visitor —or a small group of visitors—throughout his stay. Before stepping over the threshold he of course removes his shoes, which he

doesn't see again till it is time for him to leave, and he puts on one of the pairs of heelless slippers that are waiting in a row. In these he slops along behind the maid, who is carrying his baggage and leading the way to the room—or, if it is an hotel of some pretensions, the suite of rooms—allotted to him. Here he will sleep, eat and sit; Japanese hotels have no public rooms except the communal bathroom and perhaps a banquet room that can be hired by touring parties.

The way to one's room is by a succession of passages with paved or boarded floors, sometimes open to the garden on one side, sometimes simply with a view of the garden through continuous sliding windows. Every hotel is planned round a garden, which extends into bays and pockets so that the windows of each room overlook a private patch of garden. Sometimes the garden has water running through it, which the passages cross by arched bamboo bridges. Sometimes rooms or suites of rooms take the form of detached pavilions, reached by paths or covered ways across corners of the garden. The style of such gardens is too well known to need description: the various elements that make up the Japanese garden, smooth rocks, pools, plants and trees trained and meticulously shaped, are familiar the world over, cunningly placed and combined to provide balanced compositions or unexpected vistas from every viewpoint.

The layout of the hotel is inevitably a tortuous one, with many turning passages and re-entrant angles, to allow each room or suite of rooms to have a garden view without being overlooked by the windows of other rooms. Even on confined town sites such garden outlooks are the rule, though the patch of garden outside the window may be only large enough to contain a single tree, three bushes, one large stone and a little area of raked gravel, enclosed by a boarded fence but arranged to give an impression of complexity and extent.

Arriving at his own suite of rooms, the visitor will find first a little entrance vestibule, perhaps paved or cobbled, on the level of the passage he has been walking along. Here he must discard his slippers before stepping up on to the floor of the room which is covered, wall to wall, by the ubiquitous straw matting or *tatami*—the sharp scent of new *tatami* greets the visitor directly he enters nearly every Japanese hotel. When he has shuffled his feet out of his slippers the

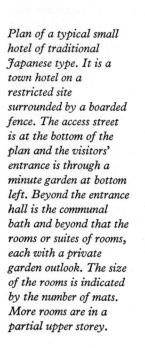

Plan of a typical small hotel of traditional Japanese type. It is a town hotel on a restricted site surrounded by a boarded fence. The access street is at the bottom of the plan and the visitors' entrance is through a minute garden at bottom left. Beyond the entrance hall is the communal bath and beyond that the rooms or suites of rooms, each with a private garden outlook. The size of the rooms is indicated by the number of mats. More rooms are in a partial upper storey.

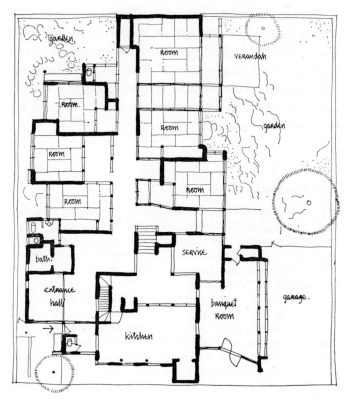

Typical room in a Japanese hotel, showing the floor covered with tatami *and verandah and garden beyond. This is in fact the Hasshokan hotel referred to on page* 115.

maid will promptly turn them to face the other way, so that they are ready for his toes to be slipped into as soon as he may want to leave his room again.

A typical suite of hotel rooms (see plan overleaf) consists of an inner and an outer room, together with a terrace or sitting-place with full-width window looking on to the garden. The rooms themselves are lit partly from this window, by means of the light that comes through the paper-covered screens that divide one room from another, and partly from panels in the ceiling, similarly formed of paper (the rest of the ceiling is probably plaited bamboo), so that the light is even in quality and comes from no particular direction.

The screens between room and room slide in overlapping sections. They are of wood, very lightly framed, so they slide easily. A characteristic sound in a Japanese hotel is the gentle clatter of sliding screens as, otherwise noiselessly, the maids go about their business. Sliding screens also conceal cupboards in the other walls, and when the screens are closed there is no way of telling where the wall opens and where it doesn't. One gets a nervous feeling that a panel in any wall of the room may open at any time and the maid pop in. In a little room off the entrance vestibule is a lavatory—perhaps a wash-basin as well, if the hotel is very up to date—and there are small circular rush mats to serve as stepping-stones across the cobbles.

The rooms have no furniture, except a low square table in the centre of the inner room, with flat cushions arranged round it,

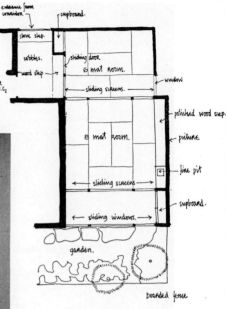

The Japanese hotel: dinner at the Torikyo Hotel, outside Atami (see page 128); the sliding screen separating the two rooms that comprise one visitor's suite is wide open; the low square table, removed when dinner is over, is the only piece of furniture. On the right: plan of a typical suite (lobby; 6-mat room; 8-mat room; verandah) in the hotel at Hiroshima. For a typical hotel exterior, see page 112.

and a folding mirror in the outer room, on the level of the floor since the user sits cross-legged in front of it. The *tatami* takes the form of mats of standard size (6 ft. by 3 ft.), bound with fabric round the edges. According to the well-known Japanese modular system, used also for the traditional-style house, the mat forms the basis of all room-sizes. The subdivisions of walls and windows, including the sections of which the sliding screens are built up, coincide with the dimensions of the mat, so that a uniform linear pattern and system of proportion unite the whole interior. In the typical suite of hotel rooms shown on the plan above, the inner room is a 6-mat room, and the outer an 8-mat room. The generous size of some hotel rooms derives from the Japanese custom of travelling in families and groups, half a dozen people often occupying one room.

The manner of life in a Japanese hotel is strictly according to custom. Immediately after showing the room, the maid produces tea and then takes out from one of the wall-cupboards a lacquer tray containing a set of robes with wide hanging sleeves: a short cotton robe, a long padded one with a sash to tie round the waist and a short outer jacket. The visitor undresses forthwith (if he is Japanese he lets himself in fact be undressed by the maid, who takes his clothes away to wash and iron), he puts on the robes and sets off to the communal bathroom, a largish room with the bath, which is permanently full of very hot water, sunk into the floor. In all but the most unsophisticated hotels there is nowadays a separate bathroom for men and women.

You must not wash or use soap in the bath since the water is not renewed for subsequent bathers. At the other side of the room are hot and cold taps projecting from the wall at skirting level, together with soap, a little wooden stool to squat on and a wooden vessel for sluicing water over one's body.

Having cleaned and rinsed oneself with the help of these, one climbs down into the bath and sits up to one's neck in the steaming water, chatting to one's friends and fellow-visitors, for as long as is agreeable. Then one dries, puts on the layers of heavy robes, which one wears for the rest of the evening, and shuffles back along the passage to one's own rooms.

The thickness of the robes is needed because the rooms have no heating—unless the weather is quite cold when a small charcoal brazier may be brought in. Private houses are equally unheated and very cold in winter, to which the Japanese are accustomed, and wear layers of thick underclothing. The central heating of houses and traditional-style hotels is almost unknown because they are built of wood, bamboo and paper—all inflammable; most types of contruction normal in the West are ruled out by the likelihood of earthquakes. Concrete, instead of timber, frames are practicable, but are not popular for domestic, hotel and similar building because the Japanese like soft wall surfaces which means a separate wall-lining, and therefore greater expense, if concrete is used. They are also domestically conservative.

After the bath—dinner, which the maid brings in and arranges on the low table in its multiplicity of little dishes. You sit cross-legged (unless in one of the occasionally-met-with luxurious rooms with a pit beneath the table containing burning charcoal in which you can dangle your legs, warming your toes and preventing the warmed air from escaping with a quilt tucked round your knees). The maid sits—or rather kneels—at table with you and whatever travelling companion may have joined you for the meal, assiduously replenishing the little china cups of *saké* and prattling away with local gossip and small-talk—to make agreeable conversation to visitors is a part of her training. The maids are mostly plumpish country girls. The hours are long—about seven in the morning until perhaps midnight—and willing girls are becoming difficult to get. But the atmosphere in which they work seems generally to be a happy one—that of a large chattering family. In one typical hotel with thirty-two bedrooms there were twenty-six maids, as well as kitchen and other staff.

Every now and then the maid leaves the table to fetch another course, involving herself in a seemingly endless process of kneeling and rising: up from her knees to carry a tray to the screen; down again to place it on the *tatami*; straighten up to slide a panel open; down to lift the tray across the threshold; up again to carry it to the outer screen and so on; a process that is repeated with every duty she performs since it is a rigid custom that she should kneel when sliding screens open or shut or taking anything up or putting it down—all done silently except for the clatter of the screens and the soft padding on the *tatami* of her white-clad feet.

In a Japanese hotel, the visitor pays for room, dinner and breakfast, but the cost is more dependent on the quality of the meals than on the room itself and the same room can be engaged at widely differing prices according to how luxuriously the visitor wants to eat. Dinner is long drawn out and afterwards it is time for bed. The maid removes the table and its cushions and, going to one of the wall-cupboards, takes out the bedding: mattress, pillows and two or three quilts. With these she makes up a bed in the centre of the room, carefully and exactly equidistant from every wall. It is comfortable enough—in fact all the arrangements are wonderfully well thought-out and comfortable—as well as visually restful because of the way this domestic architectural tradition avoids surrounding the occupants of a room with a permanent clutter of possessions. Only the Westerner finds himself conscious of the lack of anywhere to put things down in a completely furniture-less room without even a shelf. He must stoop over his suitcase on the floor; his watch and spectacles must simply be placed somewhere on the *tatami*; even the robes he is provided with have no pockets.

SIXTH DAY

UP EARLY TO CATCH A LONG-DISTANCE bus across the mountains to Hamada, a town on the opposite coast, facing the Sea of Japan—the journey from Hiroshima will take nearly five hours. Crowds in the bus terminal, lining up for the smart new buses that set off every few seconds; long-distance bus travel is an important part of modern Japanese life, and in remote places such services, many of which are run by the railway companies, are superseding the branch railway lines.

Dashing up-to-date vehicles—Japanese-made, like most of the cars in the streets —with white or shiny aluminium bodies gaily painted in the manner of children's toys with stripes and panels of primary colours. Radio music while you travel. Out of Hiroshima through the crowded narrow suburban streets—so narrow that the side of the bus almost touches as it goes by the open-fronted shops, the builders' yards, the small timber houses and workshops that line the route—no pavements in these streets. But soon country of a kind begins, though farmhouses, standing almost on the road frontage, are so close together the impression is still that of a built-up area.

A typical farmhouse enclosed by trees. The gateway leads into the garden forecourt.

A traffic-sign at the end of a village street.

Hiroshima is surrounded by pointed, forest-clad hills with power-lines strung across them, separated by broad valleys, intensively farmed. The cultivation very meticulous, as though each plant was separately tended and every square foot of ground continuously hoed. Wheat in tidy ridges; bright green patches of various vegetables, some under polythene cloches; rice-paddies terraced up the hillsides with stone-faced retaining-walls; round haystacks with a pole up the middle.

The farm buildings of timber, long and low with projecting eaves giving sheltered storage space; their roofs thatched with reeds or covered with grey or brown glazed tiles; the farmhouse itself reached through a densely planted miniature garden, with evergreen bushes and orange trees laden with fruit, the garden walled in by a wooden fence and a tall arched gateway. Few birds to be seen, and no livestock in the fields except occasionally cattle pulling ploughs and chickens in coops; no farm buildings on the land except those grouped closely round the farmhouses—every scrap of available land made use of for growing things.

A splendidly effective traffic-sign in main road villages: wherever the road turns sharply, facing the oncoming traffic stands the cut-out figure of a policeman, full-size and in natural colours, his arms raised over his head—threatening enough to cause the most impetuous driver to slow down.

The problem of rural depopulation: the young men tend to leave the primitive, laborious life on the land for the attractions of town life and industrial employment, and they are further discouraged from staying in the country by the marriageable girls being even less willing to stay. Farm life is hard for women, who have to do a lot of the work. The fields are too small, the ground too irregular, the crops too various for the wholesale mechanization that would make a reduced farming population possible. Some signs of mechanization, however, such as motor cultivators being pushed along the furrows.

Wilder country soon, with the mountains steeper and closer together as the road winds up into them; no room for cultivation except in small stream-watered valleys; deep snow by the roadside as we cross the highest pass (1,800 feet). Then down the winding, gritty road to more farmland and the dusty, unpretentious town of Hamada.

From Hamada, where the bus-route terminates, by car to Gotsu, bumping over wretched half-made dusty roads—the surfaces of minor roads, and of some main roads, are appalling in Japan but there is a big programme of arterial road construction (see the section on *Transport and Tourism*) which in a short time will bring about a great improvement.

Gotsu is a smallish coastal town with wood-pulp and rayon factories; a brief stop there to look at the new town-hall, just completed and due to be officially opened the following month. Designed by Yoshizaka, professor at Waseda University, Tokyo, it is a somewhat brutal building well sited on the spur of a hill overlooking the town. The central block loses in expressiveness by having its concrete walls rendered and painted, giving it to the Western eye something of a 1930-ish character. More successful is a wing which, dramatically suspended on V-shaped columns, projects over the hillside. The interior is gloomy but has a good entrance hall with paved floor and a staircase with a timber handrail of interesting profile.

Little cups of tea with municipal officials; then by train (one and a half hours) along the indented rocky coast to Izumo, where another famous Shinto shrine stands at the end of a grove of pine-trees. The usual barn-like buildings with vast timber roofs, projecting eaves and rafters curled up at the end; in this case the timber unpainted but touched with gold; the inner buildings dating back 200 years (though rebuilt then in a style centuries older); the most prominent building only four years old, having been rebuilt after a fire. The Japanese seem to be continually reconstructing their ancient monuments in accordance with religious custom or because they are dilapidated or have been burnt, which has happened often since all the buildings are of timber, but it never seems to worry the Japanese visitor when little that is in fact ancient remains—how different from the Western tourist where the guarantee of something being genuinely old takes precedence over the degree of interest or beauty.

Izumo Grand Shrine has the unusual interest of a modern building in prospect—

(*continued on page 61*)

A typical Japanese village, with timber-built, tile-roofed houses and shops, one or two storeys high, making a continuous frontage to the long, winding village street. This is part of the main road between Hiroshima and Hamada.

Town Hall, Gotsu

architect: Takamasa Yoshizaka

A town hall and municipal offices completed in 1962, with a two-storey wing, suspended on V-shaped reinforced concrete columns, projecting over a steeply sloping hillside. Above: from the foot of the hill. Above, right: close-up of the office wing. The dark bands above and below the windows are painted red. Right: inside the entrance hall looking down the staircase.

Right: surviving houses of traditional type along the river-bank at Matsue. Below: the keep of Matsue Castle, 1611; timber built with a stone basement: typical of the castles found in many parts of Japan—nearly all of the seventeenth century, a time of feudal warfare and the first appearance of Western military technology.

Lafcadio Hearn's house at Matsue—a typical private house of about 1810. Top: from the street (fenced-in garden and few windows looking outwards). Centre: main living-room, with the usual sliding screens between straw-matted rooms. Bottom: verandah and garden.

Left: one of the buildings at Izumo Grand Shrine: timber and thatch, typical of the pre-Buddhist style. Below: model of Kikutake's design for the new treasury at Izumo.

a new treasury to house and exhibit the shrine's various relics and antiquities—designed by Kiyonori Kikutake, one of the best of the younger generation of Japanese architects. This treasury, due to be finished in 1963, represents an unusual as well as an enlightened piece of patronage on the part of the chief priest, since religious institutions—in Japan as elsewhere—normally show very conservative taste, and the new building is prominently sited alongside the main entrance forecourt.

The chief priest, a distinguished, relaxed personality; tea with him in his office where a balsa-wood model of the new treasury was displayed: an oblong building with steeply sloping walls giving it an almost triangular section. The structure is four reinforced concrete columns between which span prestressed beams 160 feet long. The wide walls have a pattern of rectangular concrete panels with glazing between the ribs. Then to look at the site, in the company of a young assistant from

Kikutake's office; foundations poured and the column reinforcements showing as clusters of steel rods against the sky.

From Izumo on by car over even more uncomfortably stony roads. A rice-growing area, especially the reclaimed land alongside Lake Shinji, which is cut off from the sea by a narrow neck of land and which the road skirts on its southern side. Prosperous-looking farmhouses enclosed by close-planted screens of tall trees as protection against the sea-winds. Arrival eventually at Tamatsukuri, a resort standing above the lake, and the usual elaborate welcome at another—this time luxuriously planned and up-to-date—*ryokan* or Japanese-style hotel.

The main street of Yasuki, a village on the road from Matsue to Yonago.
It shows how main-road traffic has to push its way along narrow built-up
streets without even a pedestrian pavement between the roadway and the
fronts of houses and shops.

SEVENTH DAY

TO MATSUE—PARTLY ALONG A NEW toll-road; a fair-sized city (population about 100,000) sited where Lake Shinji almost joins up with an inlet from the sea; the capital of Shimane prefecture (a prefecture in Japan is roughly equivalent to an English county, or more exactly, perhaps, to a French *département*). Matsue is unusual for having been almost undamaged in the war. Most Japanese towns of any importance were half destroyed in air-raids (or rather by the fires that followed air-raids); Matsue, having been spared, preserves more pre-war character than the others and is more consistently furnished with timber houses of traditional style.

A visit first to Matsue castle, a fortified residence typical of a number to be found in Japan, mostly of the seventeenth century: multi-storey, set back at each level with gabled pagoda-like roofs; white plastered walls above a ground floor of large polygonal stones; inside, huge reddish timbers and ladder-like stairways. The castle enclosed in pleasantly landscaped grounds, reached by steep gravel paths and gateways in the surrounding wall.

From the castle across the river for a duty visit to Lafcadio Hearn's house, which has been devotedly preserved. It is looked after by an old lady who remembers him quite clearly; attached is a little museum with the touching array, usual in such places, of his manuscripts, pipes, walking-sticks and the desk at which he wrote. This most famous of the many Westerners who became Japanese scholars and devotees of ancient Japanese lore lived here when he was old, after he had married his Japanese wife and become a Japanese citizen, until he died in 1904. Though such assiduously preserved interiors, musty and little visited, are always sad places, this had the added interest of being an untouched example of the modest private house of about 1810: one-storey, timber-built, presenting a secretive frontage to the street, the rooms, one leading from the other, floored with *tatami* and looking out through their sliding screen windows on to densely planted—now rank, green and mysterious—patches of garden.

Next an utter contrast: to the centre of the town to look at the prefectural museum and art-gallery, completed in 1959—designer Kiyonori Kikutake; a highly sophisticated reinforced concrete building and, like most Japanese architecture of the modern school, showing the influence of Le Corbusier, but perhaps in this case more particularly the influence of his work in India. The main display space is one large first-floor gallery with a row of columns down the middle, lit through sliding-folding screens at either end. It stands on a triple row of columns and the space underneath is penetrated by a system of stairs and balconies, with offices at mezzanine level. The supporting structure heavier than the Western eye is accustomed to because of earthquakes; the floating planes beneath interestingly handled; a very successful entrance hall—raw concrete, brick panels, sombre cool colours, staircase to the mezzanine with shiny black pressed metal handrail. Upstairs the sliding-folding gallery windows wouldn't open or close because the winch-operated mechanism had rusted up—presumably a result of the salt sea air.

From Matsue to Yonago, past level fields, a patchwork of greens with damp brown rice-paddies and farmhouses again closely wrapped in trees. Through the narrow main street of Yasuki and soon into the outskirts of Yonago—a large town

(*continued on page* 69)

Matsue; a main street in the modern part of the city, typical—in its incoherence, its makeshift appearance and its profusion of wire and advertisements—of most Japanese towns and cities. See the comment on page 69.

64

Museum, Matsue

architect: Kiyonori Kikutake

The museum and art gallery of the Shimane prefecture, of which Matsue is the capital: completed 1960. Above: from the south-east. Below: close-up of mezzanine staircase and balconies from the surrounding garden.

Museum, Matsue

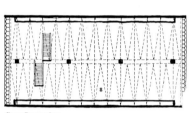

first floor plan

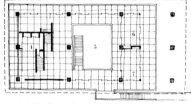

mezzanine floor plan

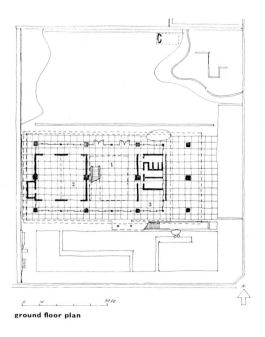

ground floor plan

0   10   50 ft

Above: the museum from the north, looking into the open lower floor. The main exhibition gallery occupies the whole upper floor of the building and is lit by sliding-folding windows at either end. These are seen closed in the view (facing page) from the east side. Below: the entrance hall and staircase.

N

key
1. entrance hall
2. lecture room
3. office
4. storage
5. upper part of entrance hall
6. committee room
7. curator
8. exhibition gallery

Auditorium, Yonago

architects: Murano and Mori

A municipal meeting and concert hall with a range of municipal offices attached to it, completed in 1960. Top: the flank wall of the auditorium, faced with red brick, and external staircase and gallery. Centre: side view of the auditorium. The foyer is beneath the upper tiers of seats on the right. Bottom: stage end of auditorium with office wing on left.

Left: glass-roofed shopping arcade off the main street of Yonago, decorated with sprigs of plastic cherry-blossom. Right: municipal offices, Yonago: typical of the better local official architecture.

(population about 80,000) chiefly dependent on pulp mills, its prosperity indicated by the forest of television aerials sprouting from the roofs of its close-packed wooden houses.

The makeshift appearance of streets and buildings which, together with the general untidiness of wire draped criss-cross and on poles up either side of the street, of rubbish and advertisements, one is coming to accept as characteristic of every Japanese town, as it sprawls untidily along its approach road; an ugliness and disorder no less evident in the centre. But by now, having been appalled by it to begin with, one is beginning to wonder whether one should be too censorious about this urban squalor—whether criticism by Western standards is justified or relevant. A much-quoted explanation of this in James Kirkup's *These Horned Islands* is that the Japanese have a sense of beauty but no sense of ugliness. That is an appealing generalization, but not wholly convincing if only because people much nearer home put up with ugly surroundings with no more complaint or evidence of being sensitive to them. But there must be some explanation beyond the absence of town-planning control, and perhaps it can be found in the meticulous tidiness of the cultivated countryside. Here everything is neat, well planned and precise, with every square foot of ground put to the best possible use. There is no sense of the freedom enjoyable in the more casual, broader spread of our own fields and woods and commons, and although the land that cannot be cultivated—the steep, rocky mountain sides, pine forests and unfertile uplands—occupies over 80 per cent of Japan, it has neither the accessibility, the variety nor the sense of being available for the ordinary person to use, of our own countryside—you can't walk over Japanese farmlands; they are nobody's playground. Outside the towns the Japanese are thus always under discipline, and only the urban scene offers a needed release, an outlet for spontaneous constructional energy, an opportunity for the enjoyment of anarchy and of the visual pleasures of accidental relationships. The towns, in fact, are their jungle.

A stop in the centre of Yonago to see the municipal auditorium, a boldly shaped structure, of reinforced concrete and pink brick infill, by Togo Murano. Like the work of some other modern architects of his generation—those who became involved in the new movement when they were already well established—it has something of an Art Nouveau flavour and also something Dutch about it: affinities perhaps with Dudok. Then a walk down Yonago's central shopping streets which have—like several other Japanese towns—glass-roofed arcades running off them, usually supported on thin iron columns, valued in summer when the temperature is suitable for strolling out of doors but rain incessant.

These arcades crowded with people and decorated with sprigs of plastic cherry-blossom, acid-pink, in anticipation of the coming cherry-blossom season—a season which is eagerly looked forward to as it draws near and the subject of endless discussion, of exchanges of mutual enthusiasm and pilgrimages to parks and public spaces noted for the richness of their display of blossom. An oddity: the models in dress-shop windows all blondes with Western features.

A glance at the municipal offices—like those at Hiroshima and Matsue, a commendably simple, modern, workmanlike building—then away from Yonago by car to the hotel at Kaike, a short distance away on the coast; another Japanese-style hotel, light and airy with long, rambling passages overlooking unusually spacious gardens; up-to-date but, like them all, wholly traditional in style and arrangement.

A curiosity in some Japanese hotels: displayed in a hall or passage is a long-tailed cock, a species of domestic fowl whose tail feathers, if given the chance, cascade downwards to a length of several feet. To exhibit this the wretched bird is imprisoned in a piece of glass-fronted furniture like an asymmetrical grandfather clock, facing sideways and perched at eye level with room for his tail to grow downwards to the floor.

A stroll down to the shore—a sandy bay, enclosed by rocks crowned with stunted pine-trees—for a view over the wind-ruffled indigo-blue sea towards the invisible coast of Siberia; then a visit to another, neighbouring, hotel, similar in style but

70

with some interesting recent additions. Kaike is a flourishing hot-spring resort, very popular with the Japanese; hence the presence of a number of up-to-date hotels. The buildings added to this one consist of a bath-house overlooking a broad beautifully planted garden and a residential wing opening off a sandy courtyard; architect, Isao Shibaoka. Both are timber-built, pleasantly and unaggressively modernized versions of the traditional style—the latter's rational, modular planning and elegant use of timber, plaster and bamboo demand nothing else.

Back to the other hotel for evening bath and dinner; the communal bathroom an unusually spacious and picturesque affair which pipes its water direct from the hot springs that emerge under the sea along this stretch of coast: a high-ceilinged room

In most Japanese cities a complex of narrow unpaved lanes enclosed by traditional-style timber houses lies immediately behind the modern blocks of buildings in even the most sophisticated central districts, retaining, as this side-street in Yonago shows, a wholly village character.

Recent additions to an hotel at Kaike; architect, Isao
Shibaoka. Left: the bath-house from the garden. Right:
corner of a two-storey bedroom wing.

with one wall all window, opening on to the garden (with a terrace outside for the
use of bathers when the weather is warm enough for throwing the window open)
and a large, irregular-shaped sunken bath, surrounded and islanded with natural
rocks. From apertures in the rocks the spring-water comes steaming out; it must
be cooled on the way, because it emerges from the springs at a temperature of
187°F.

EIGHTH DAY

FROM KAIKE TO YONAGO AGAIN to catch the daily plane to Itami airport, one hour's flight south-eastwards, which serves both Osaka and Kyoto. The usual wait in a crowded passenger hut and then a bumpy flight through thick grey cloud. No view below until we are over Itami and on the point of landing.

A typical busy, untidy provincial airport and an even untidier road to Kyoto, the main highway between the second and third cities of Japan; thirty miles of continuous shacks, factories, wire-mesh fencing, power-lines and advertisements. A poorish road, but here—as elsewhere between big cities—new motorways are under construction. Those seen, however, give the impression of being already hardly wide enough for the increasing weight of traffic.

Into Kyoto, the historic capital of Japan and seat of the emperors, a sprawling city like Tokyo but not quite so shapeless because its streets are on a regular grid plan. Right through the city to the Miyako Hotel standing on high ground on the eastern side: a Western-style hotel this time, large and anonymous of the kind you might find in any big city, and a world away from the Japanese-style inn. Instead of being populated by quiet Japanese gentlemen taking baths, it is bustling with parties of loud-voiced American tourists: business men with cameras and rimless glasses and their wives with blue-rinsed hair who call to each other like seagulls as they swoop up and down the arcade of souvenir shops.

The hotel has a recently added wing (architects, Murano and Mori) looking towards the city, with a strongly modelled, balconied façade of which the first floor is projected forward above a bare brick ground floor. From the upper windows an instructive view of Kyoto in its setting of mountains, which surround it on three sides; on the roof of the new wing a kind of Japanese-style penthouse: suites of rooms surrounding a roof-garden in imitation of the traditional hotel with its garden courts and rambling passages.

After lunch, out into the city, to look first at the one important modern building Kyoto possesses: Maekawa's *kaikan* (or festival hall). This is similar to his building for the same purpose at Ueno Park, Tokyo, even more successful from the point of view of lucidity of plan and spatial arrangement, designed just before the Tokyo one

A central Kyoto street crossing, typifying the incoherence of nearly all Japanese street architecture. On the right, surviving among the new modernistic buildings, the canopies that cover many of the pavements.

but not executed till after. It was completed in 1961.

A notably mature design, with a large and small auditorium and a conference wing, interestingly planned on two sides of a terraced courtyard. The smaller auditorium, as at Tokyo, the more successful, but natural timber beautifully used throughout the interior, for acoustic as well as decorative reasons. In the foyers, rather garish wall decorations in coloured ceramics. As at Tokyo, the foyers are finished with richly textured materials—purple-brown brick, raw concrete and paving setts in large-scale patterns—such as the West associates more with the outsides of buildings. The external proportions strong but not cumbersome; the sad colour of untreated concrete in fact not disagreeable even in dull weather; the finish of the concrete good; a copper roof to the main auditorium. The cost of the building, £800,000, raised largely by a tax added to the charge for admission to the various tourist sights (temples, palaces and the like) in the Kyoto neighbourhood, thereby permitting the old world to contribute something to the embellishment of the new.

Back past the new post-office, a very decent, if somewhat unsubtle, modern building alongside the main railway-station, designed by Ko Yakushiji, an architect in the enlightened Posts and Telegraphs Department led by Hideo Kosaka—see page 76. The traffic moves faster than in Tokyo, partly because of the less tortuous street-plan and partly because of the existence of a few really wide, double-track streets created as it were by accident; when the wartime bombing was at its height, and whole quarters of the city were threatened with destruction by spreading fires, fire-breaks were created by tearing down rows of property, and these swathes cut through the closely built-up city remain as the new highways.

Out again in the evening to a dinner-party given by the Foreign Ministry: the host Ambassador Kohno, head of the ministry's Osaka branch office. Other guests: Foreign Ministry and municipal officials; local architects Hiroyasu Tomiie and Sano, secretary of the Kansai branch of the Japanese Architects' Association.

The Japanese custom of silently and formally bowing when anyone meets anyone else. The Westerner has three reactions: as regards the moderate bow between acquaintances, he soon gets into the habit of doing likewise; as regards the much deeper bow from the waist, palms on thighs, between strangers when introduced, he is a bit nervous of this, not so much from self-consciousness as because he is

Detail of the wall and balcony treatment of the Miyako Hotel, Kyoto; architects, Murano and Mori. The hotel entrance is on the left.

75

Left: the new head post-office at Kyoto by Ko Yakushiji, of the Posts and Telegraphs architect's department.

Right: one of the wide double-track streets (the hedge seen bottom left forms the central reservation) carved through Kyoto on the site of war-time fire-breaks.

puzzled about knowing when to stop—two Japanese, mutually bowing, each one's forehead almost touching the other one's shoulder, seem to know when to straighten up again so that they do so perfectly simultaneously, though there is no sign of an exchange of signals; thirdly, as regards the obsequious bow of, for example, the welcoming hotel-keeper—down on the knees, palms flat on the ground, forehead touching the floor—at first he is embarrassed at what he feels to be an unnecessary as well as an unfamiliar gesture of servility, but soon he realizes that the gesture is based on formality and custom, and he accepts it as such—which does not however mean that he knows quite how to react while the gesture is being made.

The dinner-party held in a private room in a Japanese-style restaurant—a room glazed down to the floor along one long side and looking out on to an unusually beautiful garden. The ritual as before: cross-legged on a cushion at the low table; little cups of *saké*; the long drawn out meal of many courses served in an array of dishes and shiny lacquer bowls. But, since this is a somewhat ceremonious occasion there are, in addition, *geisha* girls whose job it is to minister and amuse.

(*continued on page* 81)

76

Festival Hall, Kyoto

architect: Kunio Maekawa

The south-east corner of the building, with the terrace outside the first-floor conference hall.

In the plans below, only the ground and first floors are shown. The second floor contains the upper part of the main auditorium, with more foyer space, and committee rooms and a delegate's lobby in the conference wing.

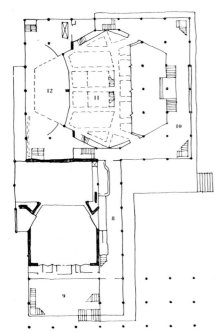

first floor plan

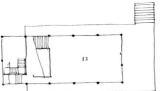

N

Above: the interior of the main foyer. Below: the main auditorium, showing the split bamboo wall-lining.

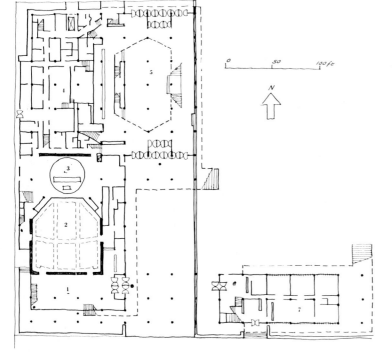

ground floor plan

key

1. foyer of small auditorium
2. small auditorium
3. stage
4. dressing-rooms, etc.
5. entrance foyer of main auditorium
6. entrance to conference wing
7. conference offices
8. restaurant
9. upper foyer
10. foyer of main auditorium
11. main auditorium
12. stage
13. conference hall

78

Festival Hall, Kyoto

Completed in 1961 and sited near the centre of Japan's ancient capital, this is the equivalent of the same architect's festival hall at Ueno Park, Tokyo (pages 32–36), except that it also contains a conference hall and offices, occupying a separate wing with their own entrance (see plans on facing page). Compared with Tokyo, the positions of the auditoriums are reversed, the small auditorium being at street level and the main auditorium one floor up. Above: from the south, showing the way through beneath the first floor between the auditorium and conference wings. Below: closer view of the centre part of the same street frontage.

Festival Hall, Kyoto

Close-up of first-floor terrace (see page 77), showing Maekawa's handling of reinforced concrete in detail.

Dressed in a traditional style peculiar to their calling, in the bright colours of tropical birds with long falling sleeves and skilfully manipulated trains; hair piled up, stuck with pins and crowned with tinsel ornaments; faces thickly powdered a matt white on to which are painted artificial eyebrows and mouths; these unreal, accomplished, doll-like creatures kneel beside the guest, replenishing his cup of *saké*, helping him to tit-bits from the dishes in front of him and making cheerful conversation in twittering, bird-like voices. Towards the end of the meal they get up and dance, to the accompaniment of the *sam-sen*, a stringed instrument like a guitar: slow, formal dances with gesturing of sleeves and fan; or they sing sad or gay little songs, returning to kneel beside the table between times.

Pretty enough in their stylized way they nevertheless—it should be said in view of the misconceptions about the *geisha* sometimes current—are (to the Westerner anyway) without much sex-appeal; their manners are so formal and remote and the white socks they wear with a separate compartment for the big toe are rather off-putting to the Western eye, looking like hens' feet as they point them outwards in the dance.

NINTH DAY

A DAY SPENT VISITING HISTORIC sites, which abound in and around Kyoto. First to Nijo Castle, right in the city, a palace built by one of the *shoguns*, Tokugawa Ieyasu, at the beginning of the seventeenth century and enlarged by his grandson, who also incorporated in it parts of a neighbouring palace a few years older. It was for the *shogun's* own use when he visited Kyoto—the *shoguns*, the real rulers of Japan, resided at Yedo (now Tokyo) while the titular emperors had their court at Kyoto.

The main group of buildings—the Ni-No-Maru Palace—consists of four square blocks staggered in plan so that they only connect at the corners, allowing each to overlook the garden—that *leit-motif* of Japanese architecture. A corridor runs round the perimeter of each; the first three contain audience chambers, with faded (but to experts important) paintings on their sliding screens; the last the *shogun's* private apartments. They are timber-framed, stuccoed buildings with heavy tiled roofs, and are enclosed by walls within which is a landscaped garden with great rocks and an irregular lake. Covering a much bigger area and enclosing also a second residence, itself protected by a moat, are outer walls with gateways and corner turrets—again of white stucco with grey roof-tiles and basements of stone—the whole surrounded by an outer moat: an impressive system of fortifications with an unusual breadth and simplicity and sense of space within.

Across the street from the castle gateway another modern hotel (architect Yoshimura, formerly professor at Tokyo University), a pile of long balconied windows towering above the narrow streets of little wooden houses and entered from the other side through a courtyard somewhat absurdly walled-in in the style of the castle opposite. From there out to the north-western edge of the city, to the Kinkaku-ji* temple to see the so-called golden pavilion, part villa, part monastery, an ornate, heavily gilded affair, looking as bright as new and in fact totally rebuilt in 1955, reputedly in fifteenth-century style; the sort of filigree architecture the Western eye finds it very difficult to distinguish from every theatrical designer's

* 'Ji' in fact means 'temple', but both words are used here for the sake of clarity.

82

idea of oriental magnificence, this one, however, having the attraction of standing in a splendid forested park.

Next, to the Ryoan-ji temple not far away; just before reaching it a new small house by the roadside in course of construction, interesting to observe because the traditional method of house-building, still in use everywhere, can be seen in detail. It is a carpentry job, with the spaces between the timbers filled with brownish mud mixed with boiled seaweed. This will later be covered with weather-boarding or plaster.

The Ryoan-ji temple (see page 86) is a monument to be taken more seriously than the golden pavilion, not only for the temple buildings themselves, which are agreeable enough examples of the gabled broad-eaved timber architecture that is the type of the Buddhist temple all over Japan—this one is pleasantly approached by steep gravel paths winding among pine trees—but on account of the famous sand-garden that lies to one side of it.

Enclosed within a mud wall, kept low on the only side from which the visitor can look into it, this is a flat rectangular area of sand studded with rocks or groups of rocks like islands in a sandy sea, the sand being finely raked in a pattern of straight lines which become concentric circles round the bases of the rocks. Created in the fifteenth century by the artist So-ami and endowed with mystical significance by the devotees of Zen, it is in fact, whether one chooses or not to read symbolic significance into the placing and relationship of the groups of stones, a three-dimensional abstract picture of wonderful calm, dignity, texture and colour.

Ryoan-ji temple, its paths, courtyards and terraces, thronged with a pushing

The new Kokusai Hotel at Kyoto,
by Junzo Yoshimura.

A traditional-style carpenter-built house under construction; note the female labour.

crowd of school-children and other visitors, mostly herded into parties by uniformed guides carrying flags so that each member of a party can easily identify his own. These highly organized crowds of sightseers being characteristic of all the architectural monuments of Japan—they swarmed too along the paths leading to the golden pavilion and occupied nearly all the available ground-space, indoors and out, at Nijo Castle—something should be said here of the remarkable part tourism plays in Japanese life and the physical form in which it is organized.

Transport and Tourism

The two go together because the transport system is bolstered financially by the tourist trade, which is a flourishing one. Historic sites and ancient monuments, together with hot-spring resorts, national parks and the like, are all crowded, largely with Japanese, arriving and departing in buses. It is as though the streams of camera-hung, guide-book-carrying visitors in Florence, Capri and Venice all turned out to be Italians.

For the Japanese are indefatigable tourists in their own country, due, one supposes, partly to a mixture of cultural curiosity and educational policy; but largely also to the fact that travel abroad is almost impossible

for financial and political reasons. Tourism is very highly organized and takes place largely in groups. Every social class participates. School-children travel round the tourist sites—the ancient castles, temples and shrines—in enormous numbers as part of their educational curriculum, though they must save up the money for it themselves.

These school sight-seeing tours, conforming to set itineraries, are adjusted as to scope and duration to suit children of different ages. At least once during their schooldays nearly all children manage to cover the

(continued on page 89)

On this and the next two pages:
historic buildings in Kyoto
representing three characteristic types.
Right: Nijo Castle, a palace built by
one of the shoguns in the early
seventeenth century—looking along
the moat to one of the gate-houses.
Below: the main entrance gateway
to Nijo Castle from within the first
courtyard.

Two more historic buildings in Kyoto, characteristic of their kind. Above: the Ryoan-ji temple—typical of the wide-eaved timber buildings of the many eighth- to tenth-century Buddhist temples in the Kyoto and Nara areas. Ryoan-ji also possesses a famous sand garden— see page 83. Facing page two: views of the Katsura Palace, a seventeenth-century imperial villa standing in a large landscaped garden.

Craftsmanlike and sympathetically designed detail, such as is found all over Japan: a high bamboo fence surrounding the gardens of the Katsura Palace in Kyoto— see the preceding page.

Monuments of Buddhist art and architecture. Left: Todai-ji temple, between Kyoto and Nara (note the crowds of sightseers which are a permanent feature of such monuments in the tourist season). Centre: the great bronze Buddha in the same temple with a touring party of schoolgirls in the foreground. Right: the early wooden Buddha at the Horyu-ji temple. See page 94 for a typical pagoda, the other type of building which, together with the barn-like halls (this page and page 86), the gateways and the treasure-houses, comprise the complex of buildings of the Buddhist temple.

whole country by means of such tours, each of which generally takes about ten days. They carry picnic meals and sleep the night at inns, which again are very largely supported by the tourist trade. They convert their larger rooms into dormitories on demand, a dozen or more children bedding down on the *tatami* together.

One cannot arrive during the travelling season at a famous Buddhist temple or Shinto shrine, whether in a city or in the depths of the countryside, without finding numbers of the special—very smartly de-signed—tourist buses parked in rows under the trees and disgorging troops of children, the boys dressed in the military-style uni-form that all Japanese schoolboys and stu-dents wear from the age of six until they leave the universities at twenty-two—black trousers and jacket, the latter fastened close round the neck, with brass buttons down the front—and the girls in their own slightly less stereotyped uniform—usually dark blue skirts and jumpers with sailor collars. There is no ascertainable reason why the boys' uniform takes it style from the army and the girls' from the navy. It is also, incidentally, noticeable that even when not in uniform very few of the schoolboy and schoolgirl generation wear traditional Japanese dress. Particularly among women, such dress is still common in the streets even of the big cities, but it looks as though within less than a generation kimono and obi will have disap-peared from the scene, except perhaps in-doors and in the remoter districts.

The touring school-children are well dis-ciplined and follow a fixed route round temple courtyard, pagoda, treasure-house and landscaped garden in compact droves, listening to guide-lecturers, photographing each other in front of memorable back-grounds and investing in souvenirs and refreshments before piling into their buses to move off in convoy to the next place of call. But although their numbers are remark-able, they provide only one element of the throngs that people every ancient monu-ment. There are similar organized parties of adults. Many Japanese people belong to clubs through which they save up money to

go on sightseeing tours, often twice a year, often five hundred at a time, chartering a whole train or a whole fleet of buses. Especi-ally addicted to this form of semi-educational amusement are farming people, who are prosperous just now owing to the Govern-ment system of subsidies. Like farmers everywhere they value good living, and so their tour programmes are also designed to allow them to sample the cooking of the region they are travelling in. Tours are also undertaken by parties of old people. It is an accepted custom to give presents to old people in the form of tickets for a sight-seeing tour.

The prosperity of the bus companies is largely dependent on this highly organized group touring industry; they have special departments to cater for it and provide uni-formed guides who carry flags so that strag-glers can reunite themselves with the right party. And since many of the bus companies are subsidiaries of the railway companies, the prosperity of the former is passed on to the latter. It provides one of the reasons why the Japanese railway companies pay their way,* a thing railways in other countries seldom manage to do, though there are other reasons too: the fact (in the case of the Japanese private railways) that they are not confined to a single activity—they run bus services and manufacture buses and rolling-stock and can therefore co-ordinate road and rail traffic to suit the economic demands of each; and the fact (in the case of both the private and the national railways) that the road-system throughout Japan is not at present good enough to deprive the railways of their profitable traffic.

It may not, however, be so for long, be-cause of the big programme of road con-struction now under way and the rapid increase in the use of motor-cars, an increase that has not in fact been deterred by bad roads—Japanese drivers subject their cars to treatment on rough road-surfaces that few other car-owners would countenance. But motor-cars will multiply as fast in the

* A new railway line is even now being built: the high-speed Tokaido trunk railway connecting Tokyo with Osaka and Nagoya.

89

country as they have done in the towns when road conditions are better.

The new roads, it may be mentioned, are, although centrally planned, locally financed to the extent that many of them are toll-roads. They will remain so only until their capital cost has been paid off. The expectation is that this will take twenty or thirty years, but in some of the toll-roads already operating, such has been the traffic that the cost seems likely to be paid off in a good deal less. The amount of the toll varies; for an ordinary car it may be the equivalent of 1s. 6d., it may be as much as 5s.

Even in the cities new road-building programmes are not inseparable from tourism; for example, Tokyo's very comprehensive programme, necessary in any case, has been given a special impetus by the coming Olympic Games. Of the twenty-three new cross-town highways planned (at an estimated cost of £130 million) eleven were designated by a traffic subcommittee of the Olympic organizing committee as being essential if the fiasco of the 1958 Asian Games was not to be repeated. On that occasion traffic congestion prevented some officials and many spectators from reaching the stadium at all on the opening day.

Some of these twenty-three highways are half built, some not yet begun, the chief cause of delay being the number of property owners who are reluctant to move—the Japanese are but slowly feeling their way towards the compulsory acquisition of land (see section on *Town Planning in Evolution* on page 117). 6,000 houses or shops stand in the way of these new Tokyo roads, and by autumn 1961 only the owners of 1,600 had signed evacuation contracts. Most of the others were holding out because they were not satisfied with the compensation offered. This is fixed by the city government on the basis of local land-values and the age of the building to be demolished, and is likely to account for seventy per cent of the whole cost of road construction.

Tourism, and the transport industry that thrives on it, is not restricted (except presumably in the case of the school parties) to archaeological and architectural sites. Other centres of activity are the hot-spring resorts and the national parks. The latter are about the only places in Japan where the countryside is accessible and people can enjoy getting close to outdoor life. The farmlands, because of the nature of agriculture—small patches of land intensively cultivated or rice-paddies perennially under water—are not accessible like the European countryside, and the only recreational use the steep, forested mountain sides are put to is a limited amoung of skiing enjoyed by the middle classes in winter-time. So in the summer season the national parks, especially those near the main centres of population, like the Ise peninsula and Hakone, draw enormous crowds.

The hot-spring resorts like Atami are very popular, not only among passing tourists but among holiday makers who, like the tourists, subscribe to clubs as a way of financing holidays there. Many trade unions run such clubs and maintain their own hostels in places like Atami (as the Russian factory unions do at the Black Sea resorts) and the big industrial corporations and some Government departments do the same, holidays there being organized on a co-operative basis.

Finally, mention must be made of the cherry-blossom season which gives tremendous impetus to tourism. It evokes fresh enthusiasm every mid-April, enhanced by local patriotism, and for a week or two half the people in Japan seem to be on the move, touring around viewing each other's blossom.

In the afternoon to the Sanju-sangen-do, a thirteenth-century reliquary or sculpture-hall built to contain a statue of Buddha and a thousand supporting gilded life-size images—which it still does, standing shoulder to shoulder like the crowds at a coronation: a simple rectangular building, whose name means thirty-three spaces—the number of spaces between the columns—claimed to be the world's longest timber building (390 feet); complex internal roof structure, the heavy members barely visible in the gloom.

Then to the Katsura Palace, south-west of the city, standing in its vast romantic garden, too famous to be described here. The building (see page 87), an imperial villa of the seventeenth century built by Prince Toshihito, has a complex plan produced, as it were, by joining asymmetrically a number of rectangular pavilions, so that as you wander from room to little room you are always turning corners and being confronted by a new outlook (through sliding window-wall or from open-fronted balcony) on to a garden vista carefully contrived to suit it. The palace is all on one level, but raised above the surrounding garden. Its plastered, timber-framed walls, beneath a half-gabled overhanging roof covered with grey-brown thatch, allow one to note for the first time the distant origin of the simple, rational Japanese domestic style with which modern architects have discovered so many close affinities.

TENTH DAY

IN THE MORNING, BY CAR from Kyoto to Nara, looking at various Buddhist temples on the way, mostly in the rain but taxis always carry paper umbrellas in the boot for the use of their passengers. At first through well cultivated country (this is one of Japan's two principal tea-growing areas), but later more forested and later still given over largely to bamboo plantations. Bamboo grown as a crop since it has many practical uses; some of these unexpected, such as the long flexible bamboos used throughout Japan for clothes-lines, where in the West we would use cord or wire. This area recently devastated by a typhoon.

Bumpy, narrow roads, made the more difficult for traffic by constant bottle-necks in the shape of the long main streets of villages, where two cars can hardly pass and where the roadway is made narrower still by deep open ditches in front of the buildings along either side. But now and then a glimpse of the improved main-road system on which work is steadily going forward, as when our road passed under the new double-track highway between Osaka and Nagoya, sweeping across the country free of intersections, one of the first sections of the programme to be completed.

Here is not the place to describe the ancient Buddhist temples south of Kyoto and in the area round Nara. They are famous monuments and every detail is given in the text-books. Anyway, to the inexpert Western eye they look very much alike. Eschewing therefore all expertise on layout, roof-construction, carving and the like—to say nothing of their sculptural contents, another expert study on its own—it can be said that their visual appeal lies chiefly in their colour—sombre brown touched with faded red, occasionally enlivened by the brightness of new orange-vermilion paintwork, against the dark greens of the fir plantations in which most of them stand—and in the subtly proportioned spaces that the ranges of low buildings enclose and partially sub-divide by means of the taller, asymmetrically placed elements like the pagodas and treasure-houses.

Again it is strange to find in temple after temple how little store seems to be set by the actual antiquity of the fabric. A building is revered as twelfth-century or whatever it may be even if it has been restored or rebuilt in quite modern times, as long as the old appearance has been exactly reproduced. The Daigo-ji temple with its miles of boundary walls—of plaster over a base of mud and bamboo, with stone bases and capped with grey tile—has a very fine tenth-century pagoda that was lately taken down and reassembled and defective parts renewed, the whole process taking six years, ending in 1954. Similarly the tenth-century Byo-do-in temple a little farther along at Uji, famous for its eleventh-century bronze bell, was dismantled and re-erected just after the war (such work, if the building is listed as a national monument and protected as such, is paid for by the Government). And the Todai-ji temple, which houses an enormous bronze Buddha, was rebuilt in the eighteenth century after a fire. Now it has a sprinkler system like a city department store which keeps its timbers damp if the temperature rises above a certain point.

Happily the finest temple of them all, the Horyu-ji temple near Nara, has been very little rebuilt. It has a complete outfit of sturdy, eighth-century buildings enclosing a courtyard of splendid proportions; also, surrounding an adjacent court-yard, a nunnery (rather rare in Japan), an austere, beautiful early wooden Buddha ('National Art Treasure No. 1'), a clumsy modern concrete treasure-house made clumsier by traditional-style curly-eaved roofs (but fortunately well out of sight)

Part of the new double-track highway between Osaka and Nagoya; in the distance, an under-pass and a by-passed village.

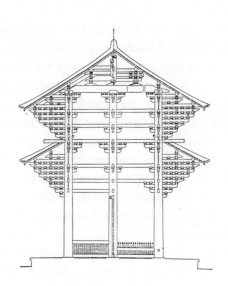

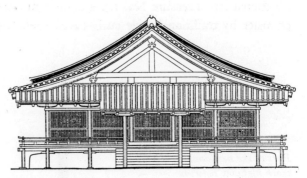

Buddhist temple architecture.
Above: a typical pagoda—at the
Yakushi-ji temple, near Nara. Above
right: section through the south
gate of the Todai-ji temple, showing
characteristic bracketed construction.
Below right: elevation of hall
at the Horyu-ji temple.

and the usual avenue of trashy souvenir-stalls and pin-table booths.

Such squalid appendages to historic monuments are another aspect of the curious contrast to be found all over Japan: reverence for beauty co-existing with frequent insensitivity to the process of desecrating it—a tendency, it must be acknowledged, noticeable in other countries as well. It is perhaps inseparable from the highly developed tourist industry which in these famous Buddhist temples is very much in evidence again. Buses full of school-children are unloading all the time, conducted parties queueing at gateways, crowds milling round each statue, pagoda and refreshment-booth, neat lines of parked buses filling every tree-lined vista.

Nara: the site of the ancient—even more ancient than Kyoto—capital of Japan, now wholly a tourist town. Not a particularly attractive one, but not too large and

94

well sited among rocky hills rising abruptly above their tree-clad lower slopes. In time for lunch at the Nara hotel, which stands on high ground at the edge of the town: a two-storey timber building, Japanese architecturally with low-pitched roof and widely overhanging eaves, but furnished and run wholly in Western style. Agreeably old-fashioned, with a spacious Edwardian air: lofty corridors lined with match-boarding; Turkey carpets, wide fire-places and basket-chairs; coils of rope outside each window for use in case of fire.

Off again in the afternoon on a sight-seeing programme which includes two more eighth-century temples (the Yakushi-ji and the Toshodai-ji) and the Kasuga Grand Shrine whose orange-vermilion buildings look almost luminous between the trees; but also, making a nice change, the modern Yamata art gallery. This is a rural gallery of Eastern art, founded and endowed by the president of one of the private railway companies, recently dead. The building was opened only at the end of 1960. It has a park-like setting of pine-clad hills surrounding a small lake, and was designed by a senior architect, Isoya Yoshida, whose previous work had been wholly conservative in spirit. An interesting, and in many ways effective, exercise in the art of architectural compromise: modern in plan-form and structure but still with reminiscences of Japanese traditional styles. The total effect is agreeable, especially the warehouse-like character of its plain walls and roofs, though it does not create a sense of leading anywhere interesting as do the more uncompromising

A Japanese example of period-style architecture: a new range of buildings at Tenri University.

concrete buildings by the architects a generation younger.

The walls a grid of concrete ribs protecting a mosaic surface in a vivid, somewhat harsh, blue-green; the interior beautiful: one large square gallery with a small garden courtyard in the centre containing tall bamboos, visible through its plate-glass walls but disappearing upwards out of sight. The exhibits—paintings, sculpture, ceramics and the like—mostly small; sparsely arranged and chosen on an aesthetic rather than an art-historical basis. The lighting and colour of the whole interior very good; also in the little lecture hall that opens off the foyer.

On the way back to Nara, a golf-course with lavish club-house—one of a great number seen from car or railway train, recalling again the new Japanese enthusiasm for golf; and not only as a sport, for to certain sections, especially business sections, of society golf is coming to mean a lot socially and even financially. The subscription to these country clubs is relatively low but the entrance fee is often around £300 to begin with and increases thereafter, and since membership is transferable it is regarded as an investment, to be disposed of profitably when the fee has gone up. Membership of a golf club is one of the things the senior employees of big commercial firms expect to be given on their expense account.

A detour to visit an architectural curiosity that is at the same time a place of some significance in Japanese life: Tenri University, the headquarters of Tenri-ko, a sect of Shintoism founded about a century ago, which is very active and propagandist and a political force throughout Japan; and indeed abroad, since there are many foreign students at the university. Attached to it is a religious centre, where a festival is held twice a year to which groups of pilgrims come, including whole families at a time, from all parts of Japan. It is housed in ranges of traditional-style buildings, and the particular architectural curiosity is the vast new training centre, completed only in 1956. This is one of the largest recent buildings in Japan, designed in a ponderous ornate style, based on reminiscences of ancient Japanese temples (architect, Professor Shozo Uchida). The five-storey building (two storeys in the roof) provides half a million square feet of floor area. An extension, providing another 150,000 square feet, is under construction in the same style. It is comforting, of course, to an Englishman familiar with the tenacity of retrograde architectural ideas, to find that in a country as modern-minded as Japan such extravagant irrelevancies also survive. In China buildings of this kind—or a simplified version of them—are, it may be recalled, of course, still the rule.

A night at the Nara hotel; surprise at seeing from an upstairs window, after darkness had set in, a blaze of coloured neon lights from a hill-top above the town—marking, it turns out, a newly installed American-style pleasure-park or Disneyland, providing the tourists who flock to this area with an alternative entertainment which must contrast very forcibly with the ancient temples, shrines and archaeological sites for which it is already famous.

96

Art Gallery, Nara

architect: Isoya Yoshida

Top: the entrance front. Above: the side of the building where the ground falls steeply to a lake, showing the link between the entrance wing (left), which also contains offices and a lecture hall, and the gallery wing (right).

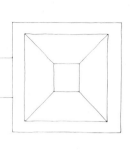

first floor plan

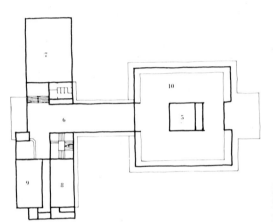

upper ground floor plan

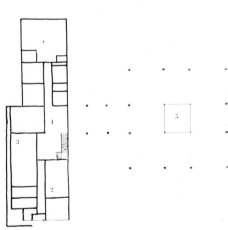

lower ground floor plan

Art Gallery, Nara

The Yamata art gallery is a private rural gallery, in a setting of water and pine trees, opened at the end of 1960. The large ground-floor gallery, surrounding a small planted garden, is approached through an entrance hall (below) off which are a lecture hall and the curator's offices. At an upper level are the stock rooms. The outside walls (see preceding page) are covered by a grid of concrete ribs backed by green mosaic.

key

1. packing room
2. offices and
   workshops
3. storage
4. machinery
5. garden court
6. entrance hall
7. lecture theatre
8. director's rooms
9. offices
10. exhibition
    galleries
11. void
12. gallery
13. stock room
14. upper part
    of lecture theatre
15. projection room

ELEVENTH DAY

NARA TO OSAKA, A DISTANCE OF twenty-eight miles by road. Round Nara is the centre of the goldfish-breeding industry and in the villages are little farms whose chief preoccupation is goldfish, whence they are exported to nearly every country in the world. Country roads again passing through the narrow streets of straggling villages; then a new toll road, well engineered though spoilt by the multiplicity of road-side advertisements. Wilder country as the road climbs upwards; flurries of snow on the pass; then the long zigzag ride downhill again to the plain in which Osaka lies. Another—quite spectacular—toll-road; more frequent advertisements; thickening wirescape; then the industrial outskirts of Osaka and soon the built-up city itself.

Osaka, with a population of over three million, is the second city of Japan, sited at the head of an inlet at the eastern end of the Inland Sea. It is the most important commercial and industrial centre, though after the war some of the big corporations moved their head offices to Tokyo to be in touch with the Government departments administering the various new economic controls. Osaka even more than Tokyo has the air of a thriving, expanding commercial city—it plays the part of Sao Paulo to Tokyo's Rio, and has much of the Brazilian city's dynamic quality.

Though it was badly damaged in the war there are few signs of this now, but few signs also, right in the centre, of the opportunity being taken to do basic replanning. The streets, and the bridges spanning the two branches of the wide river that make the central business area into an island, are jammed with traffic. Blocks keep it stationary for minutes at a time. An ingenious technique of helping traffic flow—initiated in Osaka but now being tried out in Tokyo too: a local broadcasting station gives out continuous announcements about where in the city congestion is worst, which motorists receive on their car radios and can adjust their routes accordingly.

First to the Osaka Grand Hotel: large, luxurious, international style; then, after lunch, down to the lobby to meet one of the leading Osaka architects, Tyuichi Mori, the partner of Togo Murano. With him to look at some of the new buildings —which in Osaka are not so scattered among the old as in Tokyo, giving the city

Part of central Osaka, seen from the island between the two rivers: along the river bank, surviving old-style buildings; beyond them, the new western-style buildings that now dominate the skyline.

more of a metropolitan scale and density. Tange's Dentsu building on one of the river banks, the headquarters of an advertising company, in exposed concrete with apertures punched in the façade in Tange's vigorous style; various other office buildings (illustrated herewith), some by private, some by contractors' architects, with aluminium exterior facings including one (the brand-new Shinhankyu building) in which the Takenaka Company has its own offices. Much sophisticated use of curtain-walls, in several cases quite up to Milanese standards and with the greenish glass often favoured there.

Belatedly, Osaka is taking some steps to improve the transport situation. The underground railway, built in 1952, is being extended, and some wide new boulevards have been built not far from the centre on ground cleared by war-damage. In one place the whole length of a disused canal is being filled in with a two-storey parking garage with a new roadway on top, and—since Osaka had a bad typhoon last autumn with the whole centre of the city flooded, and the basements of buildings filled with water so that plants were put out of action and they had no electricity for a month—river walls are being built higher to prevent overflowing. A problem is that the land in the city is sinking because of the amount of water that has been extracted, and it is no longer permitted to use the underground water supplies for cooling air-conditioning plants.

Street scene in central Osaka.

The Sogo store, Osaka, by Togo Murano, 1932:
regarded as Japan's first example of modern architecture.

A halt at the Sogo building, a department store designed by Murano as long ago as 1932. It has a façade of vertical fins, faced with faience, to cut off excess of light from the sales floors within, and was the pioneer modern building in Osaka—perhaps the first in all Japan, if you don't count Wright's Imperial Hotel in Tokyo. A glimpse in passing of the late sixteenth-century Osaka Castle, a larger version of the one visited at Matsue, with stones of cyclopaean size lining the moat; then to a very odd building, also by Murano: a recently built Kabuki theatre with a street façade designed—at the insistence of the owner—with reminiscences of the traditional style. How complaisant a modern architect should be when confronted by a client with such notions is a matter on which there may be different opinions, but at least Murano has extracted some entertaining plastic shapes and some gaiety of rhythm from this somewhat irrelevant exercise. The theatre itself, seating 1,000 people, occupies the upper part of the building. Beneath it are foyers, cafés and the like with a restaurant in the basement.

Back next to the hotel, and in the evening dinner with a group of Osaka architects: Mori, Masami Tokunaga, the secretary (Sano) of the local branch of the

(continued on page 109)

Office Building, Osaka

architect: Kenzo Tange

The Dentsu building in exposed reinforced concrete. Above: the main elevation facing one of Osaka's rivers. Right: detail of the corner entrance.

Top: the New Osaka building by Murano and Mori, facing a branch of the river. The bands between the windows are of yellow brick. Centre: the Shinhankyu building, faced in aluminium, and the Kansai electric power building. Bottom left: the Kangin building. All three are by the architects' department of the Takenaka contracting firm which has its Osaka offices in the Shinhankyu building. Bottom right: another curtain-wall office building for the Nihon Sheet-glass Co. This is by the Nikken design office—see the section Organization of the Profession (page 17).

Sports Hall, Osaka

architect: Masami Tokunaga

Completed 1958, for the employees of the Osaka area telephone and telegraph office. It has a flat steel lattice roof supported on four hollow concrete corner piers. Right: close-up of the all-glass façade. Below left: the interior showing the balcony which has seating for 430 people. Below right: the entrance front.

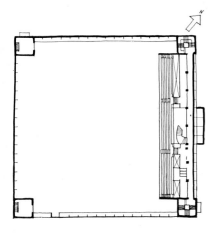

Museum, Osaka

architect: Shizutaro Urabe

The Manakata Museum is devoted to folk arts and handicrafts: three storeys of galleries, each with side lighting and the exhibits arranged round the walls and on low central tables. Above right: the entrance front. Right: the first floor gallery.

The Manakata museum, Osaka: close-up of the upper storeys, showing contrast in concrete textures.

Pharmaceutical Laboratories, Osaka

architect: Junzo Sakakura

Right: one of the wings seen from the road. Below: looking towards the main entrance which lies between two of the three parallel wings. The building, in one of the industrial areas of Osaka, is in reinforced concrete with brick facing to the end walls of each wing. It was completed in 1962.

*Kabuki theatre in Osaka,
designed in 1959 with
reminiscences of the
traditional theatre style;
architect, Togo Murano.*

Japanese Architects' Association (already met in Kyoto) and Togo Murano. Murano is one of the grand old men of modern Japanese architecture—buildings by him already seen in Hiroshima, Yonago and Kyoto as well as today in Osaka. Though seventy-one he is a man of intense vitality and alertness; his waving soft white hair and bow tie would label him a distinguished architect in any country. The conversation again reflects the Japanese architects' special concern with their status as professional men, with keeping their integrity in the face of new technical and commercial pressures (the 'package deal' in Japan is even more attractively wrapped up than elsewhere) and with all the other problems arising from the need of tried architectural methods to adjust themselves to the demands of a world involved in a bewildering process of change.

*Togo Murano, author of some of the
earliest examples of modern
Japanese architecture.*

TWELFTH DAY

IN THE MORNING MORE NEW BUILDINGS in Osaka, where the architectural standard seems on the whole higher than in any other Japanese city, as well as the central parts of the city having a more coherent and sophisticated air. Taken by Tokunaga (one of the dinner-party last night) to see a sports hall designed by him about five years ago for postal and telegraph employees—a square box glazed on three sides—then into one of the industrial areas to see an extremely impressive building by Sakakura, only just finished: a triple block of pharmaceutical laboratories in exposed concrete; gable-walls faced with brick—the influence of Le Corbusier very evident. On the way back a stop at the Manakata Gallery, a small folk-art and handicraft museum built a year ago. This is an idiosyncratic and somewhat odd building, but it has originality and character. In shape a truncated pyramid containing three storeys of galleries with long slit windows at table level on one floor and small square windows on the next; again exposed concrete, roughly textured. The architect, Urabe, is in fact the staff architect to a big rayon-manufacturing company but was allowed to take this on as a private commission because the president of the company is interested in the encouragement of handicrafts.

The afternoon spent watching *sumo* wrestling, one of the great popular spectacles of Japan. The annual professional championships were being held in Osaka. For days past the sporting pages of the newspapers had been full of descriptions of the preliminary rounds and the usual sports writers' gossip about the popular heroes taking part; the television screens had been occupied by almost nothing else. Now it was finals day, and crowds had been pouring all morning into the huge square municipal stadium, packed by the afternoon from floor to ceiling with over ten thousand excited fans.

Seats rise steeply on all four sides of the wrestling ring in the centre of the floor. Studying the proceedings through binoculars or exchanging knowledgeable comments with neighbours, munching biscuits and chocolate and sucking tinned orange-juice through straws, the spectators sit packed elbow to elbow while television cameras whirr above their heads and bright lights in a suspended canopy pin-point the sanded surface of the ring through the smoke-filled air. The ring is

Sumo tournament in progress at Osaka: in the ring, which is illuminated
from the hanging black canopy, the two wrestlers crouch, waiting for the
signal to begin.

about the size of a boxing ring but without ropes, its limits—a circle in fact as well
as name—being simply marked out on the elevated floor.

The wrestler wins when he has tipped, lifted or run his opponent out of the ring
or thrown him so that his hand or knee rests on the floor. Bouts are quick—it is
seldom more than half a minute, more often only two or three seconds, before one
wrestler is caught off balance by some unexpected thrust or hold and then the
match is over; the winner squats on his haunches on one side of the ring, the loser
bows before him and both retire. What occupies the time is the preliminaries to
each bout: a statutory four minutes during which the two wrestlers strut about the
platform, throw handfuls of salt on to the sanded surface to keep it damp with
imperious gestures like monarchs giving largesse to the poor, limber up and
observe each other according to a set ritual. Obeying the commands of the judge
who stands at the side of the ring wearing ceremonial robes and gesturing with an
odd-shaped baton (maybe a closed fan), they face each other, flexing their knees,
crouching and straightening until it is time to break off and strut stiffly about for
a little longer, airily ignoring each other's presence until the next stage of the ritual
is due. Only when the judge gives the signal for the actual combat to begin do they
become suddenly tense and spring together, gripping where they can.

The wrestlers are naked except for black cloth belts twisted round their waists and between their legs—belts ornamented with stiff archaic fringes. They are heavy men, with bulging arm-muscles and great protruding stomachs, their hair knotted on top of their heads. Contestant after contestant comes and goes, excitement mounts and shouting increases from the tiered seats as the crowd welcomes its particular heroes. And eventually the final bouts are reached in which the championship will be decided, and a rising young wrestler who has made a sensation by overturning the more noted champions day after day evokes yells of encouragement from his supporters as he flexes his muscles before facing his opponent in the last round of all. But he loses.

After the wrestling, goodbye to Osaka and a long evening journey by train and then by car to Nagoya, by way of Ise, almost on the Pacific coast, the site of one

of the oldest Shinto shrines in Japan. Its plain barn-like grey timber buildings, though replaced as a matter of religious custom every twenty years, represent exactly the archaic style of religious architecture before the introduction of Buddhism early in the seventh century. Built always of cypress wood, simple in outline, with heavy roofs whose rafters dramatically cross at either end of the ridge, enclosed in high wooden palisades, they have the calm authority of absolute functionalism before the delight in carving and ornament blurred the structural simplicity of such buildings and complicated their geometry. The road approaching the shrine lined for some miles on either side with crude concrete imitations on posts of the stone lanterns that are themselves, to the Western eye, the least appealing features of the traditional Japanese garden. These hideous embellishments—the gift of a local magnate—were proudly installed only this year. But Ise has an unusually well-designed bus station.

The railway from Osaka is a private one, the Nippon-Kinki (the same railway whose president founded the Yamata art gallery, visited two days ago); said to be the best in Japan. This particular luxury train certainly very impressive, equipped with radio-telephones and stewardesses who come round with baskets full of the customary rolled-up steaming towels. The private railways are in any case more comfortable than the national, being of the English gauge—4 feet 8½ inches; the national railways are only 3 feet 6 inches.

The train runs through plantations of small mulberry trees, grown for the silk

On the facing page: the Hasshokan Hotel on the outskirts of Nagoya; architect, Sutemi Horiguchi. This is a view from the garden of a suite of rooms with verandah, typical of the architectural style of the traditional Japanese hotel—see the description on page 49. Left: a club-house by the same architect on the adjoining golf-course, which belongs to the hotel.

industry, and later through flat, fertile plains dotted with small farms. This is a famous beef-producing region—the Matsusaka—but no cattle to be seen; they do not graze in the fields but are kept indoors all the time, fattening. Eventually to Nagoya and again for the night to a Japanese-style hotel (*ryokan*), familiar by now with life on the *tatami*, austere but refreshingly uncomplicated.

THIRTEENTH DAY

FIRST THING, A LOOK ROUND THE HOTEL—the Hasshokan—designed soon after the war by the architect Sutemi Horiguchi in a modern simplified version of the traditional style; exquisite judgment in the choice of finishes and materials. It surrounds a large garden, more open than most, with paths winding through plantations round a little lake; overlooking the lake a wing containing an unusually lofty suite of rooms and long pillared verandah added eight years ago when the Emperor came to stay. Adjoining the garden a golf-course; the club-house, also by Horiguchi, a white concrete structure dominated by the horizontal line of its flat roof cantilevered over a terrace, the two buildings illustrating the abrupt transition Japanese architecture—to say nothing of Japanese life—is at present experiencing.

Then into the centre of Nagoya—the hotel was on the edge—for a meeting with a group of the local architects in the office of the local (Tokai) branch of the Architects' Association. Nagoya, Japan's third city commercially (though in general importance Kyoto undoubtedly comes next after Tokyo and Osaka), with a population of 1,650,000, was almost destroyed in the war, having been the centre of the aircraft industry. All is therefore new, with wide main streets but the

Branch bank at Nagoya in exposed reinforced concrete, by Antonin Raymond.

Office building in Nagoya with aluminium wall-cladding; designed by the Osaka Design Office.

brashness and incoherence that at the present stage seems inseparable from Japanese city development. But Nagoya also shows some of the lively, bustling quality one was so aware of in Osaka. As with Osaka also, one is quite unconscious of being in a seaport town. Nagoya is at the head of an inlet from the Pacific, but there is no accessible waterfront; only docks and wharves on the seaward side.

A few buildings in the main streets worth stopping to look at (pages 115–116): a small branch bank, for example, by Antonin Raymond, designed in 1950, and the first building in Nagoya to treat concrete as a material that could decently be exposed; close by, a sophisticated office building with continuous windows separated by aluminium wall-cladding, designed for the Marubeni-Iida export and import company by the Osaka Design Office—an organization similar to Nikken. It seems to be these big impersonal offices with their industrial connections that are able to use Western or American building techniques with most assurance.

In the Tokai Architects' Association headquarters the conversation (with four or five architects and over the inevitable and welcome little cups of tea) chiefly on questions of town-planning and town development—not unnaturally, since Nagoya is a rapidly expanding city (its population is expected to be doubled in the next twenty-five years). Since it has recently faced the experience of almost totally rebuilding itself, the architects at least are conscious that although Nagoya made more than most cities in Japan of the replanning opportunities war damage offered, there is still lacking the will to look far enough ahead and the legislative and administrative machinery to make town-planning a positive and creative activity. This is a problem common to all Japanese cities, and may suitably be touched on at this point.

Town Planning in Evolution

The chaotic aspect of Japanese cities, described elsewhere in this narrative, and the traffic congestion prevalent everywhere, provide the visual evidence that among the most urgent needs in Japan are positive town-planning measures that go beyond the mere implementation of zoning and similar regulations. Japan has a rapidly expanding economy and is filled with industrial and commercial enterprise, which is inevitably accompanied by intensive urbanization, and this process has been so rapid that improvisation has been the only rule.

As in other countries, moreover, where the devastation caused by war has been on a catastrophic scale, the urgent need simply to get things going again—people rehoused and the wheels of industry turning—resulted in hasty rebuilding without much time to think. Only to a small degree was the opportunity taken to improve the layout of cities. There were also political factors—not only the general reluctance of a competitive capitalist economy, as in America, to let planning interfere with individual enterprise, but a special reluctance to embark on planning legislation that implied the use of dictatorial powers. After the war the re-education of the Japanese people in democratic ideals and precedures was one of the aims of the Allied occupation, and a new democracy was the basis of the constitution Japan was presented with. The lessons were learnt, leaving, however, a praiseworthy instinct against undemocratic seeming procedures. But positive town-planning, which gives first consideration to the interest of the public at large, involves to some degree riding rough-shod over private interests. Reluctance to do so shows itself in Japan in many ways. If a new city highway is planned and a single property-owner proves unwilling to sell, the project is held up because compulsory purchase would savour of past dictatorial behaviours.

This is essentially a temporary, post-war attitude, and already attempts are being made to reconcile the need for planning with democratic ways of going about it; in fact new legislation exists which includes such necessary provisions as the compulsory acquisition of property in the public interest, though these particular powers have not yet been used. It is thought they may have to be used to get some necessary new highways built in Tokyo in time for the Olympic Games—see the section (page 84) on *Transport and Tourism*.

Apart from this particularly ambitious road-building programme in Tokyo, all Japanese cities already have replanning programmes of a sort, though for the foregoing reasons they are being but slowly implemented. Tokyo is the only city to have planning legislation of a fairly advanced kind with—at least in theory—a green belt area and sites for satellite towns. In Tokyo and elsewhere there is also the usual machinery of controls, not unlike our own: land-use zoning, for example, cities being zoned, like ours, for residential, commercial and industrial use. A distinction is made between industrial and semi-industrial, and there are zones in which some flexibility of use is allowed as well as those in which the use is rigidly enforced. Such town-planning is almost wholly two-dimensional and is chiefly concerned with road patterns and land-use. There are, however, height restrictions—100 ft. is the limit in Tokyo, though special permission for higher buildings is fairly freely given in certain designated areas.

An obstacle to good long-term planning just as serious as the lack of constructive legislation or powerful political incentive, is the absence of an established town-planning profession. Those who administer the present town-planning regulations are officials who have seldom had architectural training and are not expected to concern themselves with the more positive and visual aspects of long-term planning. But this problem is now being tackled: the first course in town-planning to be available anywhere in Japan started in 1962 at Tokyo University—the State university which already runs one of the leading architectural schools in the country. The town-planning course will take four years, so by round about 1966 there will be at least the nucleus of a body of professional town-planners. An initial difficulty the university is naturally meeting is where to find teachers with the right qualifications, but this will be overcome in time.

Another requisite is of course the will to plan. This is being to some extent created by the traffic and other kinds of confusion that reign increasingly in the cities; though it is being somewhat held back by excessive departmentalism in the Government. The necessary growth of an informed public opinion has been helped by the theoretical studies put forward by some of the far-sighted architects, notably Tange's and others' plans for the future of Tokyo, and the wide publicity they have been given.

Such studies, in fact, and the research work done by groups of the younger architects like the 'metabolism' group (see pages 146 and 155), make the total picture far less discouraging than the foregoing account of the present limited town-planning activities might suggest. These researches challenge the whole conservative concept of city life on which the recent *laisser-faire* urbanization has been based. They try to face realistically the problems this process is throwing up and see the opportunity that lies in them. They furnish encouraging evidence that, in spite of being in some ways isolated from the tough world of technical and industrial development (see the section on *The Organization of the Profession*), some of the best architects openly and actively accept their profession's wide social responsibilities.

THIRTEENTH DAY (*continued from page* 116)

An excursion with a party of the Nagoya architects (Iwawo Ishihara and Hirose —first name not noted—and one of the municipal housing architects) to see some of the new buildings in the city. First a large Government office building, for the postal administration, designed by Kosaka in the fluent, sophisticated, rectilinear style that has become the hall-mark of his Posts and Telegraphs architectural office. Then to the prefectural and civic centre flanking an open grass and tree planted square—an unusual feature in a Japanese city—also designed by Kosaka though in his private capacity. He won an international competition for the building in 1954, but it was executed, without any notable departure from his design, by the prefectural government architects.

It has a well organized plan, grouped round an auditorium seating 1,300 and including also a library and art gallery. Outside, instead of the plastic, sharply modelled exposed concrete structure used by Maekawa in his equivalent buildings at Tokyo and Kyoto, it gets its character from its strongly expressed beam and post construction, with large areas of blank infill walling. The concrete frame is faced with grey brick, the infill walls are of shiny white tiles and the metal frames of the windows and glazed walls are black, giving a cool crispness to the whole composition.

Lunch in its basement restaurant, and then off to the university on the eastern edge of the city, passing on the way one of two new highways under construction that are to cross in the centre of the city—each 300 feet wide, double-track with

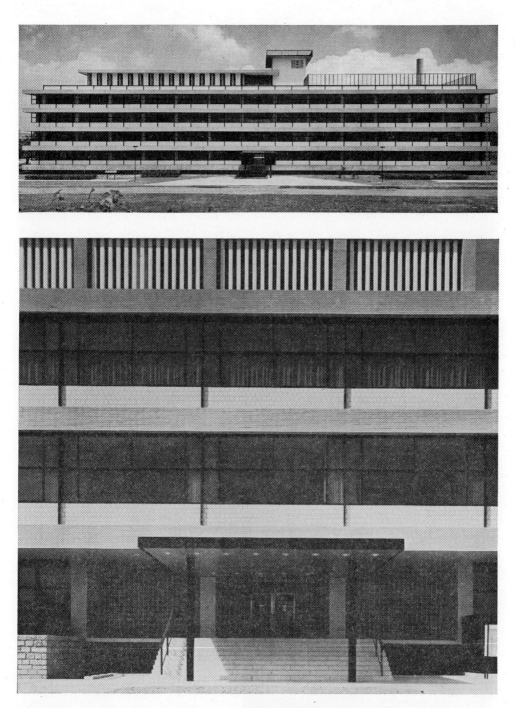

Headquarters building for the posts and telegraphs administration, Nagoya; architect, Hideo Kosaka. Top: the entrance front. Bottom: close-up of the entrance, showing brick and tile facing to the concrete frame.

four traffic lanes in each direction. A bold enterprise, though seemingly somewhat primitive as a technique of traffic planning. In spite of its wide main streets, traffic congestion is nearly as much a problem in Nagoya as elsewhere because side streets are narrow and overbuilt. There is one short length of underground railway.

Also past one well-designed high-density housing scheme, a group of parallel blocks with shops on the ground floor facing the street and an underground station beneath: concrete frame; mosaic wall-facing. It was designed by the Nikken office for the Government (as distinct from the municipal) housing corporation, which runs only a small architectural office and which puts most of its work out.

Then on to the university; dreary buildings except for the Toyoda auditorium (situated, incidentally, on the axis of one of the new 300-foot cross-town highways), which was finished the year before last and (except for a surprisingly weak and unrelated clock-tower) is one of the most impressive of the modern buildings seen in Japan. Designed by a young architect, Fumihiko Maki; in fact his first job. He was in Tange's office and is now in America—teaching at Washington University.

Besides the auditorium itself, which seats 1,600, the building contains, at first floor level, the university president's offices and a suite of conference rooms. Rising above a broad, gravelled platform, it consists of a blank-walled symmetrical block with a full-height portico at either end, each leading into the opposite end of a foyer that spans across the back of the auditorium. From the outside the porticoes give the plain rectangular building a fascinating spatial complexity, and the whole exterior is enlivened by variations of surface modelling that might be described as mannerist but are never merely affected.

This modelling emphasized by panels, high up in the wall, rendered white.

(*continued on page* 127)

Government housing at Nagoya, with shops and an underground station beneath; designed by the Nikken office.

Civic Centre, Nagoya

architect: Hideo Kosaka

A cultural headquarters for the Aichi prefecture, of which Nagoya is the capital. Instead of the more customary exposed concrete, its frame is faced in grey brick, with infill walls of white glazed tiles. Above: from the city square in front of the entrance, showing the auditorium foyer beyond the forecourt. Below: the façade from the south.

Civic Centre, Nagoya

The building contains an auditorium, a library, art galleries, conference rooms and (in the basement) a public restaurant. It was built in 1959. Above: the auditorium entrance and two-level foyer, set back behind its forecourt, photographed at dusk. The auditorium is at ground level, with concert rooms and exhibition space alongside and the library at the back. On the first floor, besides the balcony level of the auditorium, are the upper library and the art galleries. Right: a library interior.

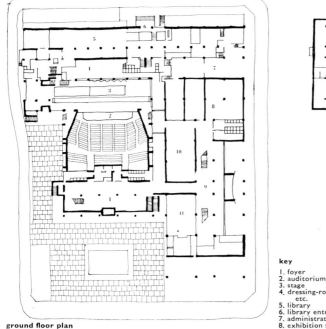

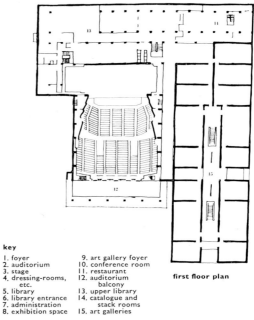

key

1. foyer	9. art gallery foyer
2. auditorium	10. conference room
3. stage	11. restaurant
4. dressing-rooms, etc.	12. auditorium balcony
5. library	13. upper library
6. library entrance	14. catalogue and stack rooms
7. administration	15. art galleries
8. exhibition space	

ground floor plan

first floor plan

Auditorium, Nagoya University

architect: Fumihiko Maki

One of the two porticos on the entrance front, facing the city.

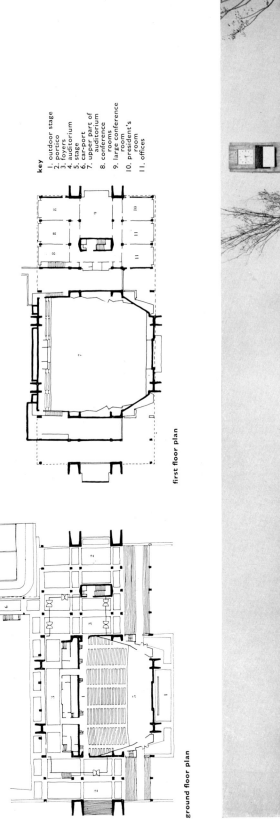

Auditorium, Nagoya University

first floor plan

ground floor plan

The Toyoda Auditorium, completed in 1961, is not only an important addition to Nagoya's university buildings, but is related to a comprehensive plan, now being implemented, to improve the eastern part of the city—the part farthest removed from the harbour—on the edge of which the university stands. The auditorium is on the axis of one of the new main highways—see page 118—and serves also, therefore, as a gateway to the university campus. It is nearly symmetrical, having a high open portico on either side of the auditorium, connected behind it by a foyer. The building is of exposed concrete, with plastered areas on the blank end wall of the auditorium and surrounding the first-floor windows. Facing page: the main elevation facing the city. Left: the side wall of the southern portico. Above: looking across and through the southern portico.

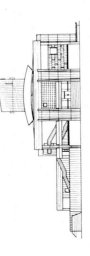

elevation

Auditorium, Nagoya University

Above: the building from the high ground to the east.
Below: inside the auditorium, looking towards the stage.

Otherwise the building is all exposed grey concrete, precise in finish and admirable in colour. Japanese critics protest that, containing as it does one great auditorium, the building should suggest this in its external form: a logical enough argument, but could one not also say that the prominence given to the two great porticoes equally—and perhaps more dynamically—suggests a building designed for quantities of people to crowd in and out? Inside, beautifully finished grey concrete too, and well-used natural timber.

From the university to see a large municipal housing scheme, also on the outskirts of the city, begun in 1949 and just completed: 2,400 dwellings (which represents a population of something over 10,000); two primary and two secondary schools; shops occupying the ground floors of some of the blocks of flats; total area about thirteen and a half acres. Architecturally commonplace and somewhat drab, it has importance nevertheless as the first effort of its kind in Japan, public authority housing on this scale being something that is only just beginning to get organized. The scheme is mostly two-storey blocks, not very imaginatively laid out in short parallel rows; some four-storey; a few point-blocks, Y-shaped in plan. All are for letting except a few detached houses built for sale.

The site covers a series of bare gravelly hills. The roads keep to the valleys, with steep paths or access roads up to the groups of houses. Construction is reinforced concrete and concrete blocks, rendered; design by the municipal housing department. Public housing in Japan is organized simultaneously at three different levels: by a Government housing corporation, by the prefectures and by the municipalities. They all have a big programme in front of them, but in spite of much primitive and congested housing, there seems to be little in Japan that could be described as

Municipal housing on the outskirts of Nagoya.

slum housing—certainly nothing like the worn-out industrial slums we know too well in the West.

Then to Nagoya railway station, to catch a luxury express (national railways) on the main line linking Osaka and Tokyo. But we are to get off at Numazu and change on to a local line which will take us across the Izu peninsula to Atami for the night. The train runs right along the coast, skirting an inlet celebrated for its eel-fisheries; through cultivated country with plantations of mandarin oranges, now loaded with fruit, and with tea-bushes climbing in long snaking terraces high up the hillsides; across wide, sandy estuaries.

Approaching the town of Shimoda, a first distant view of Mount Fuji—looking exactly like its pictures. Soon a much closer view, first on one side of the train, then on the other. Often, one is told, especially at this time of the year, Fuji is veiled in cloud, but today it stands clear against a pale blue sky, one of the few famous—and indeed hackneyed—sights that do live up to their reputation: a lofty (nearly 14,000 feet) cone, streaked with snow at the top, rising from a level plain. Its charm is supposed to lie in its symmetry, but in fact it has several irregularities, including a projecting shoulder halfway up one side; but it has a wonderful air of floating detached from the lower landscape, and enormous scale in spite of having no foothills that build up to it.

To Atami well after dark: a garish, touristy hot-springs resort, one of the largest in Japan, popular also for trade-union conferences and the like—a mixture, one might say, of Scarborough and Margate. Slow progress by car through the noisy, neon-lit streets and then, thankfully, out of the crowded town to a modern *ryokan*, the Torikyo, beautifully sited on a steep hillside on the opposite shore of the bay: architect Taniguchi, one of the architects who was at the welcoming party the first evening in Tokyo.

Only the entrance of the hotel at road level, then down flight after flight of stairs as the building steps down the hillside until it spreads out at the bottom into suites of rooms, some almost separate pavilions, planned in the usual skilful way to give privacy of outlook to each. From the windows a view across the water to the lights of Atami glittering along the shore and halfway up the opposite hill, and from the wide plate-glass windows of the communal bath a more romantic outlook still, for outside the windows is a terrace from which it seems to be but one step down to the rocks and the shimmering breaking waves.

FOURTEENTH DAY

THE VIEW BY MORNING LIGHT EVEN more glamorous than the night view promised: the bedroom window looking straight across the bay; a wrinkled blue sea and rocky headland beyond; in the foreground a grassy slope, planted with a few choice trees, going steeply down to the water. Through the sliding windows of the bedroom balcony only two steps down to the pathway of flat stones, set into the grass, that marks the easiest way to the shore—but not all that easy on *geta*, the high-soled Japanese sandals found waiting on the balcony for the visitor's use. These consist of a wooden platform with a leather strap to go across the instep and two wooden blocks beneath to keep the sandal well above the mud and wet. Peasants and old people wear them all the time, making a musical clop-clop sound as they patter along the street, but their centre of gravity is so far back that the unaccustomed wearer tips alarmingly forward as soon as he tries to walk.

The sun is warm and the air still, suitable for strolling by the shore wearing only the hotel bathrobe, a pleasure that the chilly winds of the preceding days had made impossible. But no excuse to linger now, because Kenzo Tange has promised his company for this last day's journey back to Tokyo and is waiting at the hotel in Atami where he has been staying overnight—the Atami Gardens Hotel to which he has just added a five-storey wing.

So goodbye to the Torikyo (with a present from the proprietor on leaving of an elegant box containing two pairs of inscribed chopsticks, one a size larger than the other—his, as it were, and hers; the hotel is a favourite one for honeymoon couples to whom these boxes are presented as souvenirs); then back along the cliff-top road to Atami and a view, as one turns the headland, down to the waterfront: the sharply curved bay with its sandy beach lined with tall white hotels like a transplanted segment of the front at Weymouth. Up through the town to where the Atami Gardens Hotel stands on high ground: traditional style, but standing still higher beyond its thickly planted garden is Tange's new wing looking over the older hotel and the brown tiled roofs of the town to the sea.

Beautifully finished concrete again, straight from the plywood shuttering though the arrises are so precise the shuttering might have been sheet-metal: a cool grey colour. The deeply recessed balconied front rises like a cliff above a broad paved terrace adorned with ceramic sculptures and mosaic wall-decorations by Sofu Teshigahara, known as a master of flower arrangement but recently turned sculptor; their forms somewhat bulbous and colours garish—gay and holiday-like in effect but not really worthy of Tange's subtlety of form and judgment.

Inside the hotel (a very luxurious one) the Western style predominates, but the Japanese style preserved for some of the rooms, spacious and beautifully furnished by Isamu Kenmochi, a designer who often works for Tange. Coffee in the bar, a charming room with the centre of the floor sunk one step down so that visitors unaccustomed to chairs and tables can perch comfortably round the edge.

Then off in the car on the long road back towards Tokyo, with various buildings marked on the map to be looked at on the way. The road mostly along the shore, through young fir plantations to protect the farmlands from the sea-winds; partly on one of the new toll-roads, with a very good surface but none too wide. First call—for lunch—at the Totsuka country club, one of the most lavishly appointed of the new golf-clubs that are springing up all over Japan (entrance fee said to be £1,000) and the club-house Tange's newest job—barely finished. It stands on the highest point of the bare, heathery landscape in which a 36-hole course is still being laid out and shows Tange at his most sculpturally uninhibited.

It has a huge inverted shell roof, supported on six reinforced concrete columns, and an elegant aluminium curtain-wall, with steel members introduced for wind-bracing. Over one half there are two levels: a restaurant above and locker-rooms below; leading off the locker-rooms at the end of the building, a bath-house with wide views over the mountain landscape. The other half is one great space from the floor to the underside of the upward curving roof: a hall, with lounge and bar in a partial mezzanine—the whole space handled with Brazilian bravura and furnished, like Tange's Atami hotel, by Isamu Kenmochi; the interior air-conditioned.

A long dusty drive through the same sort of country, but villages now more frequent. We are travelling over the historic Tokaido road which students of Japanese prints will remember as the subject of several famous series by Hiroshige, depicting the stations on the road where travellers stopped to change horses and litter-carriers, rest and eat. The next stop in the outskirts of Yokohama, where Yoshinobu Ashihara has built (completed 1959) a handsome and workmanlike municipal hospital. Nearby another rather interesting group of buildings: offices, club-house and youth hostel belonging to the Yokohama municipal sports association, designed in the municipal architect's office. An obviously deliberate attempt to devise a modern version of the traditional Japanese style that has really come off: one of the few buildings seen, outside the range of timber-framed domestic

(*continued on page* 139)

Hotel, Atami

architect: Kenzo Tange

The partly covered terrace; the bedroom floors above look over the town to the sea. The sculpture is by Sofu Teshigahara.

Hotel, Atami

This addition to the small, traditional-style Atami Gardens Hotel (shown shaded on the plans) has views across the town to the sea over the tiled roof of the old hotel building. The bedroom floors (the upper four) are divided into three blocks, each with three suites (some furnished in Western style, some in Japanese) surrounding a lift and stair core. The lower floors have a banquet-room, tea-room and games-room and a large terrace, partly under cover. Above: from the rear. Facing page, top: the upper (bedroom) floors facing the sea. Facing page, bottom: interior of one of the bedroom suites—tatami on floor in the foreground. Below: the bar with sunk floor.

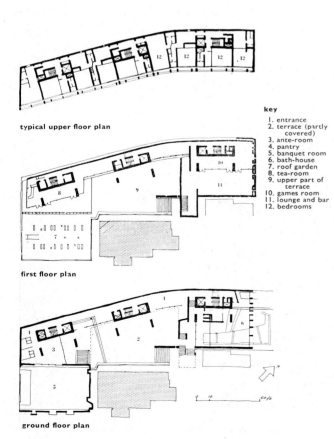

typical upper floor plan

first floor plan

ground floor plan

key
1. entrance
2. terrace (partly covered)
3. ante-room
4. pantry
5. banquet room
6. bath-house
7. roof garden
8. tea-room
9. upper part of terrace
10. games room
11. lounge and bar
12. bedrooms

Golf Club-house, Totsuka

architect: Kenzo Tange

The club-house from the south; a concrete shell roof covers the whole building.

*Left: the first-floor roof terrace outside the lounge.
Centre: the lounge balcony with the roof terrace on
right, showing one of the columns that support the roof.
Right: a column on the entrance side.*

The whole building, except for the single-storey bath-house projecting at the western end, is covered by the upward-curving shell roof, supported on six reinforced concrete columns. Inside is a two-storey hall, lounge, restaurant and locker-rooms. The building was completed in 1962. Above: a distant view of the building from the south, with bath-house on left. Below: an air view. The approach to the building is at top-left of the photograph, by way of a forecourt with sheltered parking areas. The golf-course is off the photograph on the right. Facing page top: the outside terrace and stairs. Facing page centre: staircase up to first-floor lounge; entrance screen on right, foyer to locker-rooms on left.

Golf Club-house, Totsuka

first floor plan

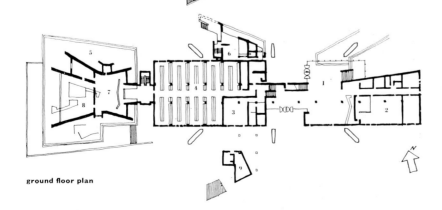

ground floor plan

key

1. entrance hall
2. administration
3. ladies'
   locker-room
4. men's locker-room
5. terrace
6. showers
7. lavatory
8. communal bath
9. caddies
10. restaurant
11. kitchen
12. lounge
13. bar
14. upper part of
   hall

City Hall, Yokohama

architects: Murano and Mori

Completed in 1960, and the outcome of a competition, it occupies a central site and contains the city offices and a first-floor auditorium. Much of the ground-space is given to a large columned citizens' hall. Above: the south façade in exposed concrete and red brick.

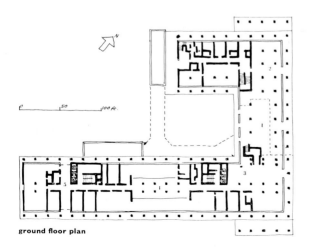

ground floor plan

key

1. citizens' hall
2. foyer to auditorium above
3. public entrance to city offices
4. exhibition hall
5. officials' entrance
6. city offices
7. auditorium

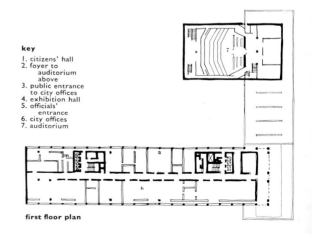

first floor plan

buildings, where modern and traditional are in effect one.

Before entering Yokohama itself, a detour down to the ancient coastal town of Kamakura (now a residential area for Tokyo), to see Junzo Sakakura's prefectural art gallery (1952)—one of the four significant early works of modern Japanese architecture (see page 47). A symmetrical building, elegantly proportioned and detailed, standing by a lake in a densely wooded park; planned round a central courtyard, open to the outside where it is entered by a wide flight of steps. Unlike the other pioneer modern buildings it is not of concrete, structurally, but has a steel frame with the upper storey, containing the galleries, cantilevered out, faced with concrete panels with aluminium trim. The ground floor in a tufa-like stone, resembling the stone Frank Lloyd Wright used in the Imperial Hotel at Tokyo.

From Kamakura on into Yokohama, a seedy, wind-blown, unattractive city now. Before the war it was outstandingly civilized and cultured, being the main gateway to Japan from the outside world. But that role is now played by Tokyo, and Yokohama has run down, becoming more like an industrial suburb at the entrance to Tokyo Bay, though preserving its entity as a city and having in fact a population of nearly a million and a half.

Buildings near Yokohama for the municipal sports association, comprising offices, club-house and youth hostel.

Municipal hospital, Yokohama, 1959; architect, Yoshinobu Ashihara.
Above: view from the west. Below: the ramp up to the main entrance.

And it has some good buildings: notably the concert hall and library by Maekawa, another of the early classics of the modern movement (finished 1954), in a simpler, more rectilinear style than Maekawa's later works, with the two elements of the building connected by a bridge; and the city hall by Murano and Mori (1959), a tall square block with an exposed concrete frame with pink brick infill, and a somewhat hard, semi-industrial character, but fine in scale. Inside, good public spaces, finished with hard, well-textured materials like stone setts and roughish tiles, somewhat sad in colour; tile murals by Murano himself.

Two early classics of the modern movement in Japan— see also page 47. Left: art gallery at Kamakura, 1952, by Junzo Sakakura. Below: concert-hall and library, Yokohama, 1954, by Kunio Maekawa.

The Silk Centre,
Yokohama, by Junzo
Sakakura, 1959. Above:
the frontage facing a
city square. Right: from
the fourth-floor café,
with view over the
harbour and its shipping.

Also the Silk Centre in the harbour quarter, almost on the waterfront, a handsome building, likewise finished in 1959, by Sakakura. The lower part contains showrooms, conference rooms and so on connected with the silk industry; the upper part an hotel, in the form of a square tower perched in the centre of the wide rectangular block. Concrete frame and panel construction; exciting view from the roof over Yokohama harbour and an impressive quantity of ocean-going shipping anchored in the roads or crawling in and out.

Away from the Silk Centre as darkness falls and up the long, crowded road to Tokyo: an hour's drive through thickening traffic towards the sparkling neon-signs and dimly seen transmitting towers that identify the central Tokyo skyline; eventually to the Imperial Hotel, which now seems quite like home.

FIFTEENTH DAY

ANOTHER DAY WITH TANGE; first to his office in Shibuya, a Tokyo sub-centre, as it might be Kensington High Street or Camden Town; its core a busy square, dominated on one side by a glass-fronted department store by Sakakura, with which is combined an elevated suburban railway station. Nearby, facing a wide boulevard, a tallish rectangular office block with Tange's office—about twenty assistants—occupying the whole of one upper floor.

Discussion with him and his partner Kamiya about various of their projects, including two alternative schemes for the buildings they are designing for the 1964 Olympic Games in Tokyo: a covered swimming-bath with seats for 15,000 spectators and a small sports hall beside it. One scheme very plastic in form with a dished roof supported on catenary steel cables; the other more angular with a folded slab roof and the spectators grouped into triangular compartments of raking seats. Drawings of a civic auditorium, already nearly finished, at Nichinan in the southern-most island of Kyushu, with a foyer partially tucked under the upward slope of the back of the auditorium, and the one-pitch roofs of stage, tower, foyer and auditorium making a series of intersecting angles.

A model in the office of a building in Tokyo for the Dentsu Company, for whom Tange's riverside office building in Osaka was designed, now at the working-drawing stage: a long rectangular building, raised off the ground, spanning between two towers containing lifts and service core and cantilevered beyond them; in reinforced concrete, but with the main longitudinal beams in steel to minimize depth; the façade in the form of a large-scale criss-cross grille, forming a kind of structural *brise-soleil*. This building, as well as others of Tange's, designed in conjunction with one of the two structural engineers of advanced ideas who have greatly helped the modern Japanese architects to achieve their free, adventurous structures, much as Arup and Samuely helped the modern English architects. His name, Tsuboi; the other, Yokoyama, works a good deal with Maekawa.

Lunch in the office—sent up in steaming lacquer bowls from a restaurant on the ground floor—with Tange and Kamiya and two architects of a slightly younger generation: Kiyonori Kikutake and Masato Otaka. Together with Maki (of the

144

The Shibuya district of Tokyo. Below: an air view
showing Sakakura's store building combined with an elevated
railway station. Above: a side view of the store.

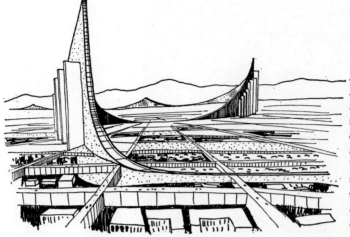

A sketch from Noriaki Kurokawa's contribution to 'Metabolism' (1960), illustrating his conception of the future form a city like Tokyo might take: a 'wall city', based on the use of the 'equipment wall' and transportation by monorail and moving corridors.

Nagoya auditorium, now in America) they are probably the best of the younger architects; those, that is, of round about thirty-five, one generation after that of the three leaders of the modern movement in Japan: Maekawa, Tange and Sakakura. Kikutake (his art gallery at Matsue already seen) has been practising on his own for a little while; Otaka has only just set up, was previously in Maekawa's office.

Both are deeply involved in theoretical study and research. Here can be found the serious thought about long-term problems that seems to be lacking in many parts of the Japanese architectural scene. Looking to the future, they and their like are an important element in Japanese architecture, with the potential influence that the English architects of CIAM had at the time when modern architecture in the West was finding its way, just before and just after the war, towards a conception of architecture that included some responsibility for the total physical environment.

One of their activities has been the formation, in 1961, of a study and research group under the name 'Metabolism' (the name indicating their vision of human society as a developing vital process), the founding members of which were Kikutake, Otaka, Maki, another young architect (and protégé of Tange's), Noriaki Kurokawa and a young critic, Noboru Kawazoe (already met when first in Tokyo at the *Shinkenchiku* lunch). This group has already published a small book on 'proposals for a new urbanism' containing city-planning projects, experiments with new types of urban conglomeration and the like, and individually—with support and encouragement from Tange—they have produced a number of impressive studies in housing and town-planning.

Energetic exchanges of views of these subjects over lunch; then off (still with Tange, Kikutake and Otaka) to look at more new buildings in Tokyo that shouldn't

(*continued on page* 155)

Flats at Harumi, Tokyo, by Kunio Maekawa—see also overleaf.

cross section

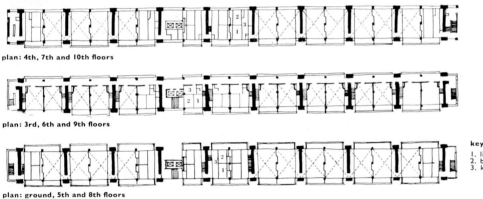

plan: 4th, 7th and 10th floors

plan: 3rd, 6th and 9th floors

key
1. living room
2. bedroom
3. kitchen-dining room

plan: ground, 5th and 8th floors

Flats, Harumi, Tokyo

architect: Kunio Maekawa

A ten-storey block built experimentally by a housing corporation in 1958 in the Harumi area—an industrial and harbour area of Tokyo. Below the penthouse, three different floor-plans are each repeated three times—see plans above—giving the balconied façade-pattern seen on page 147. The cross-section at top is approximately twice the scale of the plans. This was meant to be the first of a series of such blocks, but subsequent building followed a different pattern—as shown by the photograph (right) of one of the later blocks, and the air view (at top) of the completed scheme.

Trade Fair Buildings, Tokyo

architect: Masachika Murata

A centre for international and other trade exhibitions, completed in 1959. It consists of three halls (see site plan on right) and a block of administrative offices. Below: entrance side of hall no. 1, a square curtain-walled building with the steel roof mainly supported by a central row of V-shaped concrete columns. These also support a gallery seen on the right in the interior view (bottom photograph). The roof is also tied down at each end by precast concrete posts with tension wires between. Engineer: Yoshikatsu Tsuboi.

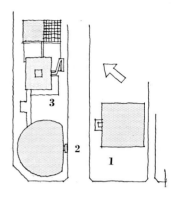

site plan

Trade Fair Buildings, Tokyo

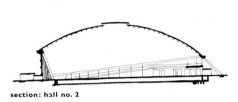

section: hall no. 2

Top right: hall no. 2 (see site plan on preceding page): a concrete shell with lattice-steel structure beneath. Height to top of dome, 103 ft. 6 in.; floor area, 117,000 sq. ft. Right: the interior, looking towards the entrance.

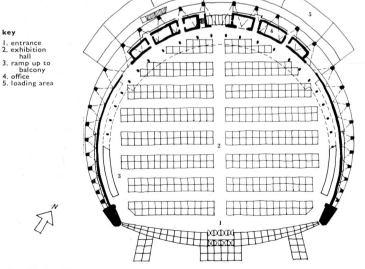

key

1. entrance
2. exhibition hall
3. ramp up to balcony
4. office
5. loading area

N

plan of hall no. 2

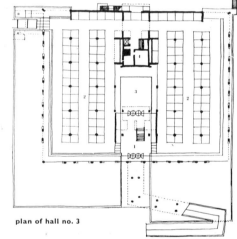

plan of hall no. 3

Top: hall no. 3, raised on concrete columns and reached by a ramp. It is connected with hall no. 2 (facing page) by a bridge. Left: staircase and corner of entrance foyer in hall no. 3, with external pool (bottom left in the plan) carried through the glazed screen into the hall.

Sogetsu Art Centre, Tokyo

architect: Kenzo Tange

A building, completed in 1957, devoted to the art of
flower arrangement, with teaching and display
accommodation: in the basement a lecture hall; on the
ground and first floors, exhibition space; on the top
floor two class-rooms (see plans on facing page).
Below: from the garden court on the south side.

second floor plan

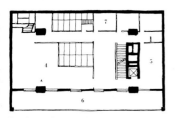

first floor plan

Above: the north side of the Sogetsu Art Centre. It is faced with dark blue tiles.

Below: an air view of Hosei University, Tokyo, where a large group of buildings (architect, Hiroshe Oe) was completed in 1958. (See also overleaf.)

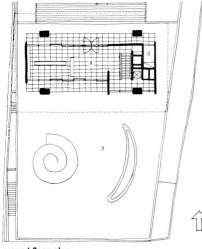

ground floor plan

key
1. entrance hall
2. caretaker's flat
3. garden
4. exhibition gallery
5. director's office
6. balcony
7. offices
8. classrooms

Interior of a students' hall at Hosei University, Tokyo (see the preceding page).

be missed. First to the Harumi area, an industrial one near the harbour, where Maekawa was asked in 1955 to design, by one of the semi-official housing corporations, an experimental multi-storey block of flats—experimental because at that time there was very little being done (there is still not much) in the way of high-density low-income housing in tall blocks, and because the earthquake problem made other countries' experience inapplicable. This block was built, and is a good example of Maekawa's vigorous handling of structural concrete, but for some reason the experiment was not followed up, and the estate was later developed with five-storey blocks (Maekawa's was ten-storey) of very poor quality architecturally.

Then to the Hitotsubashi secondary school where Kikutake has recently built a gymnasium with concrete external walling to which he has given a pattern by using diagonally placed shuttering boards (Le Corbusier's use of rough boarded shuttering to give a tough character to his concrete has not generally been followed in Japan, where exposed concrete is for the most part smooth and geometrically precise); and from there to Tange's Sogetsu Art Centre, a school of flower arrangement with lecture room, exhibition hall, etc.: a compact, square, three-storey building behind a paved forecourt, with its cross-beam construction crisply emphasized and infill walls of dark blue glazed tiling.

Then to the Trade Centre by Masachika Murata, a large group of buildings for trade and industrial exhibitions, consisting of three large halls, one covered by a vast saucer dome of steel-mesh supported by a concrete shell with zigzag struts, obviously influenced by Nervi, and a two-storey brick and concrete administrative block; the whole very competently designed if somewhat cold, with a character hardly at all Japanese. The engineer responsible for these quite ambitious structures, Yoshikatsu Tsuboi.

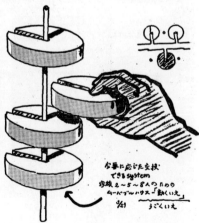

Above: gymnasium by Kikutake (1961) for the Hitotsubashi school, Tokyo. Right: diagram by Kikutake for 'Metabolism' (the publication of the research group of that name) showing city buildings formed of interchangeable circular dwelling units.

From there to Hosei University where Hiroshi Oe has built a group of vigorously modelled, well-sited buildings (about the only good modern buildings at any of the Tokyo universities—except Gakushuin, see pages 25–28); then back towards the centre of Tokyo to see one of Tange's best-known buildings, his city hall (that is, city offices), the first important modern building in central Tokyo, completed in 1956 (see page 48): seven floors of offices above a high open ground floor; a grid of black-painted steelwork superimposed on the emphatically horizontal concrete façade pattern.

Other buildings noted in passing: one for the Swedish Embassy, by the Swedish architect, Nils Ahrbom, working in co-operation with Maekawa, the result an amusingly well-balanced mixture of Swedish and modern Japanese styles; the neat but somewhat dull Nikko Hotel by Ashihara; a more ambitious modernistic hotel, but well done of its kind, by Sato Takeo—Tokyo has a vast programme of hotel building, inspired of course by the forthcoming Olympic Games, which will, by 1964, increase the capacity of the Western-style hotels in the Tokyo-Yokohama area from just over 7,000 beds at present to about 14,500.

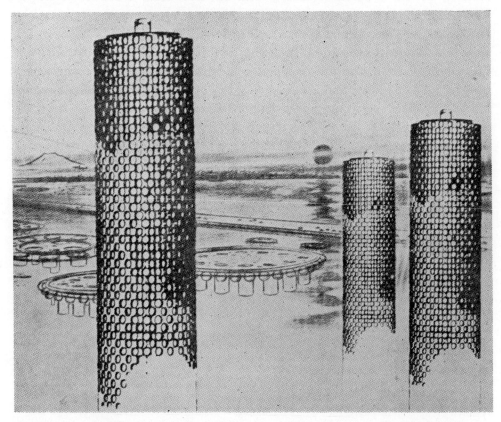

Another sketch by Kikutake for 'Metabolism': a marine city with tower-shaped communities.

SIXTEENTH DAY

IN THE MORNING TO WASEDA UNIVERSITY, which has one of Japan's two best architectural schools, the other being at Tokyo University. Most of the leading modern architects were at one or the other. Waseda has very drab buildings, designed for the most part by the university's own building and maintenance staff, but happily there has lately been a change of policy and new buildings, of which a number are in prospect, will be designed in the architectural school.

Received by two members of the staff (no students about, it being vacation time): Nobuo Hozumi, a young assistant professor with an American background—he did a post-graduate course at Harvard and then worked with Saarinen, part of the time on detailing the Grosvenor Square embassy; Naibu Akashi, who runs a busy practice as well as teaching. He has just finished a lively looking industrial building with an exposed steel frame, roofed by a series of flat domes—a foundry for casting motor-car parts—in a Tokyo suburb—see page 185.

A tour of the school and a sight of some of the students' work; also of Akashi's office and the office of one of the senior professors, Professor Imai—away just now—who is building Gaudi-like churches at Nagasaki. Professors at Waseda have office space in the school, and the assistants working there are largely post-graduate students. As well as building, they do quite a lot of research and development work—in fact this is the principal place where such work goes on. The professors' offices can afford to spend time on research because their post-graduate assistants are not fully paid, being still at the university on fellowships and grants.

The students' work very like the equivalent work of English students. The interests of the more advanced students centres at the moment, it seems, on three things: the relation between buildings and groups and the rethinking of urban structures generally (signs here of the influence of Kikutake's and Otaka's 'Metabolism' group); problems of industrialization, especially those related to the distinction, which is thought very important, between the changeable and the permanent elements in any structure; the assimilation of Japanese regional traditions into a valid modern idiom.

A long discussion about architectural education, then and at lunch. This in the staff refectory—joined for lunch by Shindo Akashi, Professor Akashi's father (formerly also a professor at Waseda, now retired, his opinions those of an older generation but he himself refreshingly open-minded and tolerant about developments he finds unsympathetic), and Bunji Kobayashi, professor of the history of art at the School of Technology, Nihon University, another of Tokyo's architectural schools, translator into Japanese of Pevsner's *Outline of European Architecture* and himself the author of a useful little book on historic Japanese buildings.

The systems followed in the architectural schools, the standard of education reached and its influence on standards in the profession are so important in Japan just now that they are worth going into in some detail.

Architectural Education

The surprising thing is that the original impetus of the Japanese architectural school system was English. In 1874 an English architect called Josiah Condor, who had been working in Japan and had acquired a great local reputation, founded the first school of architecture, on the model of the existing English schools, at Tokyo University, and Japanese schools have been run very much on English lines ever since. A statue of Condor stands in one of the Tokyo University quadrangles.

There are as many as forty or fifty universities in and around Tokyo of various kinds and origins. Most of them are private foundations, some very ancient. About twelve have schools of architecture. Waseda (on which these notes are based, though the pattern is much the same elsewhere) is one of the largest. Two or three others are about as large. Tokyo University, which vies with Waseda for leading place among the architectural schools, is relatively small. It cannot afford to expand so much because it is a State (as distinct from a private) university and has to charge much lower fees.

Waseda has about 180 students in each year. The course is one of four years—this is standard for all architectural schools. The staff would like to see it extended to five years but there are difficulties in fitting this into the university system and curriculum as a whole. At the end of the four years the students who pass out, taking their BA degree, are then eligible to sit for the Government examination qualifying them to practise as architects. But they must have two years of office experience first.

This is the normal method of acquiring the necessary licence to practise, and the method by which nearly all first-class architects qualify—see the section (page 17) on *The Organization of the Profession*. In theory it is possible for them to take the Government examination without having taken a university course and degree, if the candidate has had eight years of office experience, but in practice this is rarely done.

Waseda (and most of the other architectural schools) have ten times as many applicants for entry into the first year as they can accept. They therefore have a stiff entrance examination, about which there is the usual worry that the only practicable academic tests may exclude outstanding potential architects with a background or temperament that makes an academic examination no true test of their quality. The students pay fees—though not excessively high ones—except for about ten per cent who have Government scholarships. At Tokyo University, since it is a State university, the number with such scholarships may be as much as twenty, or even twenty-five, per cent.

Much of the first-year course is given over

At Waseda University. Left to right: Naibu Akashi, professor in the architectural school; Professor Bunji Kobayashi, of Nihon University; the author; Shindo Akashi, formerly professor in the architectural school.

to general education and mathematics, plus drawing and the history of architecture; no designing is done before the second year. After the second year, students tend to divide themselves into two streams, those that intend to specialize in technical subjects—structure, services and so on—and those specializing in architectural design (the future first-class architects). Here is the peculiarity of the Japanese architectural schools, and one of their weaknesses in the sense that standards set in the schools inevitably influence standards accepted in the profession.

All the schools of architecture in the universities are part of the faculty of engineering, and the architectural course caters for, and gives a degree to, students of whom a great many become what we might rather call building engineers. Although the Government examination covers design as well as techniques, and candidates take the same examination whichever they have specialized in during their university course, the standard of design in the Government examination is low. It has a distinct technical and practical bias. Though many of the so-called qualified architects therefore have more the character of building engineers, it should be made clear that civil engineering as such is a separate profession. The civil engineers have their own schools and their own examinations, within the same engineering faculty.

In certain specialized universities—which are in fact more what we would call colleges of technology—such as Nihon University in Tokyo, architectural and civil engineering students share the same first-year course. Otherwise there is very little collaboration between one department and another—let alone one faculty and another. Because of the extent to which purely technical skill and knowledge are accepted as the basis of an architect's qualifications, integration of the different disciplines, which

English architectural education is now seeking to increase, may be said already to exist; and because of the tendency in Japan for the building industry to overwhelm the architect as an independent professional man (again see the section on *The Organization of the Profession*), closer ties with industry are not at this stage desirable. The need in Japan is therefore, in a sense, the opposite of that in England. The need is to separate the strictly architectural disciplines from the others.

Hence the importance of the graduate schools. After the standard four-year course, Waseda (and some of the other leading architectural schools) have a two-year Master course, followed by a two-year Doctor course. Not many students, of course, can afford to continue with these, and such additional courses do not assist qualification to practise through the Government examination—in fact they delay it by delaying the statutory completion of two years of office experience. But, however small their numbers, the students taking post-graduate courses have a significant role to play. They are drawn, of course, from those who have specialized in design rather than techniques, and it is by way of their programmes and studies that higher architectural standards can be put forward. They also provide the link with the more advanced and responsible élite of the profession: the members of the Japanese Architects' Association.

As compensation for delay in getting their licences to practise, students who have taken post-graduate degrees can usually claim higher starting salaries when they come to work in offices, and many of them also gain office experience while still taking their advanced courses, by serving as assistants in the offices which many of the university professors run in the school of architecture premises. This most of the universities give their professors facilities to do, though not all take advantage of it.

At Waseda and Tokyo Universities especially there seems to be a free and adult relationship between students and staff: much mutual criticism and exchange of opinions and arguments, including inevitably, as just now in England, much discussion about the methods of architectural education. Theories and ideas are freely canvassed, and on the need for a number of improvements—especially improvements in aesthetic and professional standards—both staff and students in the more enlightened schools of architecture fervently agree.

To get substantial changes made is more difficult, partly because the present courses are part of a fixed university curriculum and partly because they have to be directed towards enabling the student to pass the Government examination. It is the scope, the balance and the standard of this external examination that need improving, but this is outside the control of the universities. They are not even represented on any board of control, as the English schools of architecture are represented on the Board of Architectural Education. The Government examination is the direct and sole responsibility of the Ministry of Construction.

SIXTEENTH DAY *(continued from page 158)*

In the afternoon, a call on Antonin Raymond. Logically some observations on his work should have come much earlier in this narrative because he is in many ways the father of modern architecture in Japan. He was Czech originally, but went to America in 1910 at the age of twenty and eventually became an American citizen. He worked with Cass Gilbert and then at Taliesin with Frank Lloyd Wright, and when Wright came to Tokyo to build the Imperial Hotel, arriving on the last day of 1919, he brought the young Raymond with him to act as his chief assistant on the job.

When the hotel was finished Raymond stayed in Japan and set up on his own. He had a small practice, mostly domestic, but built a hospital and one or two churches as well—all far more advanced than anything even being thought of in Japan. His own house, built in Tokyo in 1923, was the first building in exposed reinforced concrete. Among the young Japanese who worked in his office was Kunio Maekawa. During the war Raymond was back in America, but he returned to Japan in 1947 (to find his pre-war buildings virtually all destroyed) and now has a biggish practice and an office with fifty or sixty assistants—a practice in which his wife shares, especially over matters of interior and furniture design. In other respects, too, his office is unusually self-contained: he employs his own engineers, heating specialists and so on along with his architectural assistants, all of whom are qualified—no draughtsmen are employed as such.

Raymond's house and office are combined: a wide-eaved, one-storey timber building of his own design, planned round a garden court; his own studio-living-room opening on to a terrace and then a garden of mature trees. In spite of his seventy-two years he has a vigorous, confident personality, holding strong opinions about the shortcomings and wrong-headedness of others. In a surprising variety of ways he has had a profound influence on the development of modern Japanese architecture; not only was he the first to introduce many Western techniques and demonstrate their aesthetic implications, but it was to some extent he who discovered for the Japanese the timeless significance and contemporary validity of their own architectural traditions, especially those of their timber-built domestic architecture. The basic virtues of the best vernacular architecture have never been better described than by Raymond himself in a dialogue with Kenzo Tange published a little while ago.

'Imagine my surprise on arriving in Japan'—this was in 1920—'to find here expressed in Japanese farms and Shinto shrines like Ise, all the features which we so ardently desired to re-create in the new architecture. A Japanese farm at the time of my arrival in Japan forty years ago was a marvel of integration, complete, and perhaps not to be found anywhere else in the world. It grew out of the ground like a mushroom or a tree, natural and true, it developed from the inside function absolutely honestly; all structural members were expressed positively on the outside, the structure itself was the finish and the only ornament, all materials were natural, selected and worked by true artist artisans; everything in it and around it was simple, direct, functional, economical. The people, their dress, their utensils, their pottery, paintings, gardens, all expressed a marvellous unity of purpose clearly developed through ages by a natural process like anything else in nature. . . . It contained absolute principles, which always were and always will be the same, immutable, unchangeable and which must guide us in trying to attain true beauty in architectural design.'

After tea and conversation with Antonin and Noemi Raymond, a walk with him round the office looking at some of the projects on the drawing-boards: houses,

St. Anselm's Church, Tokyo, by Antonin Raymond, 1955—the first example of folded slab construction in Japan. Right: the exterior. Below: the interior, looking towards the altar. Facing page: the north wall.

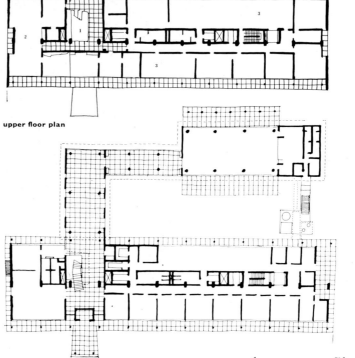

upper floor plan

Reader's Digest, Tokyo

architect: Antonin Raymond

Japan's first post-war building —it was completed in 1949— designed according to the modern architectural precepts already established in the West. Top: the frontage to the street. Centre: end of the building showing how the upper floor is cantilevered from a row of central columns but is also supported at the outer edge on steel columns sloping inward.

ground floor plan

churches, the inevitable golf club and a large scheme for a new university at Nagoya; also photographs of his just completed Gunma music centre at Takasaki, with large fan-shaped auditorium. This is Raymond's own contribution to the growing body of work by modern architects in Japan that exploits the geometrical complexities of new types of reinforced concrete structure—unfortunately too far from Tokyo to be visited now.

Then off on a tour of some of Raymond's Tokyo buildings accompanied by Hiroshi Misawa, a young critic now working with him, and Michael Czaja, an assistant professor at Berkeley University, California, who is temporarily doing the same. First to a couple of Roman Catholic churches: St. Anselm's at Meguro, finished in 1955, with the first folded slab roof in Japan; window-frames and railings of prefabricated reinforced concrete sections; furnishings also by Raymond and Noemi Raymond. Then St. Alban's at Mami-ana, also 1956; this time a timber building with an open roof economically contrived out of scaffold-poles bolted together; looks remarkably Japanese to anyone who didn't know that it would not in fact have been done like this by Japanese—an illustration of Raymond's instinctive apprehension of the real nature of the Japanese tradition.

Then to some flats he built for the American Embassy in 1952, in six-storey blocks, simple and well detailed; and finally to his Reader's Digest building of 1949, the pioneer modern building in post-war Japan. It faces the Hirakawa Gate of the Imperial Palace and is an interesting, clearly articulated design in the form of a long low block with a main first-floor slab cantilevered outwards from a double row of reinforced concrete columns, but also partly supported along each outer edge by thin steel columns which slope slightly inwards; louvred *brise-soleil* protecting the fully glazed windows of the offices above.

Then back to the Imperial Hotel, but away again almost at once to a farewell dinner in a Japanese-style restaurant given by the Foreign Ministry: the guests an agreeable mixture of officials and architects (including Tange and Maekawa). A last

Model for a new university at Nagoya, on which Raymond is now working.

St. Alban's Church, Tokyo, by Antonin Raymond, 1956—wholly in timber. Left: gable end and porch. Right: the interior.

Staff flats for the American embassy, Tokyo, designed by Raymond in 1952.

experience of the now familiar dinner-table ritual: the stresses and strains of the cross-legged posture, steaming hot towels, china cups of *saké* continually replenished by watchful serving-maids, growing pride in one's expertise with chop-sticks, Geisha girls again, doll-like, artificial and anxious to please, their dances and songs accompanied by the *sam-sen*. Back late through a city that even at night seems as packed with people and vehicles as it is in daytime.

SEVENTEENTH DAY

PACKING; TELEPHONED GOODBYES; the car-haunted courtyard of the Imperial Hotel in the morning sunshine, its textured brick and stonework looking warm and solid in the brittle surrounding townscape. Then the long dusty car-ride to the airport; the usual alternation of queueing urgently to deal with formalities and waiting idly for the next thing to happen, staring out of the window at the construction work on new airport buildings and the multi-coloured aircraft with their tall tail-fins towering over everything in sight, like giant stranded tropical fish.

Off at last—this time by the South-East Asia route. The steep climb up into the cloud-flecked sky; the banked turn giving changing views of industrial landscape, wharves and shipping and the serrated shore of Tokyo bay; an island with a live volcano—our route takes us right over the crater, but the view into it obscured by curling brownish smoke—then the straightened course in clear blue weather along the southern coast of Japan.

The sea like obscured glass, with square-sailed junks standing in towards the shore. Thick layers of cloud, but a wonderful sight to starboard: snow-capped Mount Fuji rising solitary above the cloud like a cone-shaped island in the sea. The last sight of Japan: its southern fringe of islands seen through breaks in the clouds. Then south-westwards over the ocean.

Formosa invisible under cloud. Four hours after leaving Tokyo—Hong Kong. Low cloud over the Peak; the mountain-circled harbour, crowded with shipping; the airport inevitably under reconstruction. The remarkable growth of the colony in the last ten years, especially on the Kowloon side, the vast new public authority housing schemes climbing like perforated cliffs above the waterfront, built to the astonishing density of 2,000 to the acre—even Dolphin Square is only 430.

Next stop Singapore; flat bright-green jungle with broad waterways; the curious pattern of hill terracing, like a maze in a child's puzzle-book, as we turn to land. Monsoon weather here. Then over the ocean again; Colombo after dark, but warm and humid at the palm-fringed airport; Bombay seen only as chains and clusters of glittering lights as far as the horizon.

EIGHTEENTH DAY

STILL DARK AT BEIRUT; then a grey European dawn. Frankfurt next, and as the Boeing 707 climbs steeply into the wet sky on the last leg of the flight homeward, the only task remaining, before subsiding into the semi-coma a long night of air-travel induces, is to try to dig out from a myriad of confusing impressions of modern Japan and its architecture those that are unique and essential to it.

Streets teeming with people, polite, disciplined and purposeful, familiar with every up-to-date gadget but still charmingly carrying their possessions in knotted coloured handkerchiefs (*furoshiki*, they are called); the impetuous traffic, especially motor-bicycles; wirescape and the makeshift appearance of city streets; the minute meticulous scale of agriculture, looking more like extended kitchen gardens than arable farmland; the beautiful quality of the light that comes through paper screens. The tenacity of surviving domestic traditions, shown both in the cohesion of family life and the conservatism of its architecture (though the passing visitor sees disproportionately little of the private side of life, so this aspect of the architecture is perhaps too little represented in the foregoing narrative); the civilized ritual of the Japanese-style hotel—still an authentic way of life although (one mustn't deceive oneself) in less than a generation it may become a way of life only kept going so that tourists can sample 'the real Japan'.

Gardens, of course, lovingly planned and cared for, incorporated in every building scheme however densely used the ground-space, and obviously close to the hearts of nearly all Japanese people, though the visitor trying to take in a whole national scene in a couple of weeks finds the famous Japanese gardening occupying an unexpectedly minor place in it, as also do the much publicized arts of flower arrangement and the formal tea-ceremony, which determine the whole character of Japan for the readers of American women's magazines.

Children in great numbers, more emancipated than their uniforms might suggest, so rapidly detaching themselves from old habits and traditions that they will soon be hardly distinguishable, in their tastes, values and amusements, from any children in the Western world, especially American children. Already they are noticeably taller than their parents, which scientific opinion attributes to their legs growing longer because they spend far less of their lives sitting cross-legged on the *tatami*.

And as to architecture: it may be a truism that Japan is a country in transition, but in architecture it is also a quite inescapable circumstance. Not only are Western techniques, experiences and methods of building organization being even more energetically assimilated than in the past, and creating numerous vexing problems as part of the process, but the programmes architecture has to fulfil are in transition too. For example the question is often asked how soon the powerful, elaborately rationalized tradition of Japanese domestic architecture is going to re-emerge in modern guise, but the only answer can be that while ambiguity continues in the way houses are used—while Western furniture is still in the process of being introduced to confuse the ritual of Japanese-style living, while Japanese who live mostly in Western style still have one or two rooms in their house that they use in Japanese style, while the older generation conforms to one set of rules for dress and decor and domestic routine and the younger generation another—no clear-cut architectural solution can be looked for.

Nevertheless, out of the confusing, contradictory, changeable Japanese scene a nucleus of new buildings has already been created which, individually and collectively, makes a positive, original contribution to the world's architecture. Although the modern movement in Japan is only thirteen or fourteen years old, such buildings as those by Maekawa, Tange, Sakakura and their followers, to which special attention is given on these pages, have a maturity and sophistication unexcelled anywhere. What is more important, there is no pretence of finality in the achievement they represent; they are rather, in their Japanese context, a first breakthrough, the vital initial establishment of a modern design method and a recognizable modern aesthetic that can open the way for any number of subsequent developments—technical, industrial, sociological—and eventually, perhaps, for the broader conception of architecture's responsibilities in the fields of housing, town-planning and the like, that Japan now lacks. But with the energy and initiative being applied to fostering it, this is a conception Japan will not lack for long.

THE ARCHITECTS

*Biographical notes on some of the leading modern architects
practising in Japan, printed in order of seniority, and accompanied by
pictures of characteristic buildings of theirs not included in the
foregoing pages.*

Antonin Raymond, b. 1890

The father of modern architecture in
Japan. He was born in what is now
Czechoslovakia, educated at the University of Prague and went to America
in 1910 where he entered the New York
office of Cass Gilbert, who was then
working on the Woolworth Building.
Raymond supervised its construction.
He returned to Europe in 1914, and
worked as a painter in Italy where he
met Noemi Pernessin, who became his
wife and who ever since has been his
architectural partner also. He returned
soon to New York and was invited by
Frank Lloyd Wright to join him at
Taliesin. He stayed there for a year,
leaving because Jacques Copeau offered
him the job of remodelling the Garrick
theatre, New York, for the French
theatrical company *Le Vieux Colombier*,
a venture backed by the French Government. After serving in the US Army he

*Pre-war buildings by Antonin Raymond. Above: the
house he built in Tokyo for his own use in 1923—the
first example of exposed reinforced concrete. Left:
chapel for the Women's Christian College, Tokyo,
1934, showing the passing influence of Auguste Perret.*

Antonin Raymond

French India, and from there returned to America, where he worked until 1947. In that year he came back to Japan where he has practised ever since. His first job was the *Reader's Digest* building in Tokyo, 1949, whose local influence is noted on page 165. Other buildings, apart from several houses and his own combined house and office in Tokyo, 1952 (page 161), include a bank in Nagoya, 1952 (page 115), staff flats for the US Embassy, Tokyo, 1952 (page 167), a number of churches (see pages 162, 163 and 166), a library for Mitaka (Christian) University, Tokyo, 1959, and the Fuji country

Antonin Raymond's newest building—the Gunma music centre at Takasaki. Below: the entrance and the auditorium in use. Facing page, top: the flank of the building showing the exposed reinforced concrete structure. Facing page, bottom: inside the foyer.

returned again to Taliesin in 1919, at Wright's invitation, to work on the designs for the Imperial Hotel, Tokyo. At the end of that year he accompanied Wright to Japan and stayed while the hotel (page 14) was erected. He set up in practice on his own in Tokyo and was one of the first to see the relationship between Japanese vernacular architecture and the modern ideas then emerging in Europe. Raymond's work was at first strongly influenced by Wright and then by Auguste Perret (he acquired a young Czech assistant, Bedrich Feurstein, who had been a pupil of Perret). Especially in the Perret style was the first large job he was given, St. Luke's Hospital, Tokyo, 1928. He also had in his office a number of young Japanese architects who became leading figures in the modern movement in post-war Japan, among them Junzo Yoshimura and Kunio Maekawa. Other jobs by Raymond at this time included a school, the Women's Christian College and several houses. Among the last were a house for himself in Tokyo, 1923, which was the first example of exposed concrete in Japan, and a country villa for himself at Karuizawa, 1933, with the main structure in timber and one-way pitched roofs covered in thatch, which was illustrated and admired all over the world. In the 1930s he also built a number of churches.

In 1937 he left Japan to design a dormitory building in Pondicherry, in

club, also 1959. His latest job, and one of his largest, is the Gunma Music Centre, a prefectural concert-hall and theatre at Takasaki.

Togo Murano, b. 1891

One of the Japanese pioneers of modern architecture. He was at Waseda University in Tokyo, but worked thereafter in Osaka where he started in practice in 1929 (after working in the office of Setu Watanabe) and where he has had his office ever since, though he has built in many other cities as well. In 1925 he designed the Sogo department store in Osaka (page 102), which was certainly the first modern building in that city and probably (if Frank Lloyd Wright's Imperial Hotel at Tokyo is discounted) in the whole of Japan. He has also designed, in recent years in conjunction with his partner Tyuichi Mori, department stores in Tokyo, 1957 (also for Sogo), and in Nagoya, the municipal auditorium at Yonago (page 68), the Roman Catholic cathedral at Hiroshima, 1955 (page 46), city halls at Yawata, 1959, and Yokohama, 1959 (page 138), a library for Kausai-Gakuin University, 1959, extensions to the Miyako Hotel at Kyoto, 1960 (page 75), the New Osaka office building, 1961 (page 104), and a twelve-storey Literature Building for Waseda University, Tokyo, 1962. Murano also designed recently (1959) in semi-traditional style, at the request of the client, a new *Kabuki* theatre in Osaka (page 109). In 1962 he succeeded Maekawa as president of the Japanese Architects' Association.

The Sogo department store, Tokyo, by Togo Murano and his partner Tyuichi Mori, 1957.

Sutemi Horiguchi, b. 1895

Another of the pioneers. His work serves as a link between the earlier exploitation of the modern elements in the traditional Japanese vernacular and the post-war modern idiom, his particular endeavour being the reinterpretation of the timber traditions of frame construction. He has written a number of books of which the first (published 1925) was *Modern Dutch Architecture*, in which he introduced some of the European *avant-garde* work of the time to Japan. This book was the outcome of a journey to Europe which he made soon after completing his studies at the Imperial University, Tokyo, in 1920. He visited the *Bauhaus* and was particularly impressed by the work of the *Stijl* group in Holland. Before the war his practice was chiefly domestic. Since the war he has designed buildings for Meiji University, Tokyo (where he has been professor since 1949), the Japanese pavilion for the Sao Paulo biennale and the Hasshokan Hotel and adjoining golf club-house at Nagoya, 1958 (pages 51, 112 and 113).

Yoshiro Taniguchi, b. 1904

Professor at the Imperial University, Tokyo (where he was also a student), since 1943 and, like Horiguchi, important as a link between the newer school of modern architects and the more conservative school that based its work more directly on Japanese vernacular traditions. He is also a writer. He has designed buildings for Keio University, industrial buildings at Chichibu, 1956, a number of houses, including a group of weekend houses at Karuizawa, an hotel outside Atami (page 128), the Unknown Soldier's tomb and memorial alongside the moat of Chiyoda Palace,

Tokyo, 1959, and (with Hideo Kosaka, Hajime Shimizu and Noboru Iwama) the new luxury Okura Hotel in central Tokyo, 1962.

Junzo Sakakura, b. 1904

The third of the trio of Japanese architects, the other two being Maekawa and Tange, who have led modern Japanese architecture towards its present high standing in the world. His ideas, and his handling of reinforced concrete, remain closest to those of Le Corbusier, in whose office he worked for eight years, 1929–37. Previously he had been at Tokyo University, but in the school of fine arts, not the school of architecture. While in Paris he designed the

An end view and the entrance front of Hajima city hall, by Junzo Sakakura, 1959.

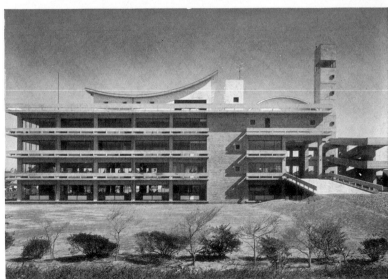

Above: group of ten weekend houses at Karuizawa, by Yoshiro Taniguchi, 1956, arranged in two terraces. Each has a verandah facing south over a shared garden.

Japanese pavilion at the 1937 Paris exhibition, which first introduced modern Japanese design to the West.

Sakakura's first important building in Japan (like Maekawa and others he spent the war years in Manchuria) was the severely classical art gallery at Kamakura, 1952, one of the pioneer modern examples—see pages 47 and 141. He was also one of the executive architects for Le Corbusier's Museum of Western Art in Ueno Park, Tokyo, 1959 (page 29). Other buildings: Hajima city hall, 1959; Yamate high school gymnasium at Ashiya, in Hyogo prefecture; civic centre, Ueno; municipal gymnasium, Seijo; Silk Centre at Yokohama, 1959 (page 142); department store at Shibuya, Tokyo (page 145); pharmaceutical laboratories, Osaka, 1962 (page 108); Kure city hall, 1962.

Kunio Maekawa, b. 1905

Has done more than anyone else to establish modern architectural concepts in Japan and has been (along with Tange and Sakakura) the pioneer among Japanese architects of the expressive use of reinforced concrete, which is Japan's special contribution to the modern architectural idiom. This work is strongly influenced by Le Corbusier, in whose office Maekawa spent two years (1928–30) after graduating from Tokyo University. On returning to Japan he worked with Antonin Raymond and at the same time formed a group of young architects to study

and propagate the ideas he had learnt in Paris. He set up independently in 1935, but his career was soon interrupted by the war.

His first important building was the concert hall and library at Yokohama, 1954, for which he won a competition. This is one of the four classics of the first days of modern architecture in Japan—see pages 47 and 141. Other

Above: two views of Kure City Hall, by Junzo Sakakura, 1961.

Below: exterior (side wall) and interior of the auditorium at the Setagaya community centre, Tokyo, by Kunio Maekawa, 1959.

buildings: flats at Harumi, Tokyo, 1958 (page 147); cultural centre at Fukushima, 1958; community centre, Setagaya, Tokyo, 1959; festival hall, Ueno Park, Tokyo, 1960 (page 32); festival hall, Kyoto, 1961 (page 77); buildings for Gakushuin University, Tokyo, 1961 (page 25); cultural centre, Okayama, 1962.

Maekawa was also one of the three executive architects (along with Sakakura and Yoshizaka) for Le Corbusier's Museum of Western Art in Tokyo, 1959 (page 29), and the architect of the Japanese pavilion at the Brussels exhibition of 1958. Until 1962 he was president of the Japanese Society of Architects—see page 16. He visited England in 1961 as leading Japanese delegate to the International Union of Architects' sixth congress in London and is a member of the IUA's executive committee.

Masachika Murata, b. 1906

Was at Tokyo School of Art and then studied architecture, first as a pupil of Shibichiro Okada and then with Kameki Tsuchiura. He then went to Europe, and although he did not work there as an architect, his subsequent work in Japan has more in common with contemporary European styles and is less evidently Japanese than that of most of the architects whose work is shown here. He was in Manchuria during the war and set up practice in Japan afterwards, beginning with an office building in Yokohama. He specialized in country clubs and hotels (Aichi: Oyamadai, Tokyo; Nagoya, 1954; Kirishima, 1957) until he was appointed architect to work with the engineer Yoshikatsu Tsuboi on the large group of buildings in Tokyo for international trade fairs, 1959—see page 149. Murata also designed the Tokyo municipal swimming stadium at Sendagaya, 1958, and is now working on a secondary athletics stadium for the 1964 Olympic Games at Komazawa Park, Tokyo.

Junzo Yoshimura, b. 1908

A specialist in domestic work and interiors, having begun as a student of Japanese historical traditions at Tokyo art school. He worked in Antonin Raymond's office in Tokyo and then, in the early war years, in Raymond's New York office. He stayed some years in America, designing among

other things an exhibition house at the Museum of Modern Art, 1954. On his return to Japan he became professor at Tokyo College of Art and has designed a number of houses, a hospital at Kambara and the Kokusai Hotel in the centre of Kyoto, 1963 (page 83).

Isao Shibaoka, b. 1911

Studied at Tokyo University and has been in private practice since 1949. He has specialized in housing, and has designed several housing schemes for the employees of industrial companies (at Yonago and on the northern island of Hokkaido, 1952; at Makiyama, 1953; at Fukuoka, 1956). These gave him more scope for dealing with the layout and grouping of buildings than has come within the experience of most of the modern architects. Other buildings include hospitals and a cultural centre for the Tochigi prefecture, and additions to an hotel at Kaike (page 72). His houses include his own house in Tokyo, which also contains his office.

Tsutomu Ikota, b. 1912

Studied at Tokyo University. Went to America in 1951 and taught at various universities. On his return he became a professor at Tokyo University and translated several important architectural works into Japanese, including books by Lewis Mumford and Le Corbusier. The practice that he combines with teaching is chiefly domestic: private houses and housing schemes in Tokyo, Yokohama and neighbourhood.

Hideo Kosaka, b. 1912

The outstanding official architect in Japan, though he has also designed a number of important buildings privately. He has been a senior member of the architects' department of the Ministry of Posts and Telegraphs since 1937 and its director since 1954, and it is due to him that postal buildings in

Postal and savings office, Kyoto, by Hideo Kosaka, 1955.

Japan have an architectural quality found in no other Government buildings. He studied at Tokyo University, graduated in 1935 and spent a short time in Matsuda's office before joining the postal ministry.

The most important postal buildings for which he has been responsible are at Kyoto, 1955, Sapporo, 1957, Hiroshima, 1958, and Nagoya, 1959 (page 119). Buildings by Kosaka of other types include insurance offices at Sendai, buildings at Tokyo airport, 1955, a department store at Komatsu, the Aichi prefectural hall and art gallery at Nagoya (page 121) which he won in competition in 1954 but which was executed by the prefectural government architects (completed 1959), and the Foreign Ministry building in Tokyo, 1960, the first central government building in a modern style. He was part-designer (see under Yoshiro Taniguchi) of the new Okura Hotel in Tokyo, 1962.

Kenzo Tange, b. 1913

The best known outside Japan of the modern Japanese architects and one of the three leading members of the movement that has placed Japan on the international map during the last ten years, the others being Maekawa and Sakakura. As well as through his buildings,

Kenzo Tange.

Tange has exercised influence, especially on the younger generation, as a writer and teacher (at Tokyo University), and through his planning studies, such as his development plan for the Tokyo area (first published in *Shinkenchiku* in March, 1961, and then, in English, in

Above: the south-east corner of the City Hall, Kurashiki, by Kenzo Tange. On the facing page: the south front of the same building (top) and the ground floor lobby (below).

pamphlet form). He lectured in the USA (Massachusetts Institute of Technology), 1959–60.

He studied at Tokyo University (1935–38 and 1942–45), after which he worked in Maekawa's office. His first completed building was an exhibition gallery at Kobe, 1950; his most important early building the memorial hall at Hiroshima (pages 47 and 49), designed in the same year, which is the first of the four buildings that pioneered the exposed-concrete, Le Corbusier-influenced style. Another was his Tokyo city hall of 1955, which he won in competition (page 48). Other buildings: his own house, Tokyo, 1953; library for Tsuda College, Tokyo, 1953; assembly halls at Matsuyama, 1953, Ichinomaya, 1953, Bisai, 1957, and Shizuoka, 1958; town halls at Shimizu, 1954, Kurayoshi, 1956, Imabari (his birthplace), 1958, and Kurashiki, 1960; printing works at Namazu, 1954, and Haramachi, 1955; Sogetsu Art (flower-arrangement) Centre, Tokyo, 1957 (page 152), Kagawa prefectural offices, Takamatsu, 1958; office building, Osaka, 1960 (page 103); hotel, Atami, 1961 (page 131); Rikkyo university library, Tokyo, 1961; country club, Totsuka, 1962 (page 134); Nichinan cultural centre, Kyushu, 1962. Winner (1962) of a limited competition for a new cathedral in the Bunkyo district of Tokyo; the other competitors: Maekawa and Taniguchi.

Tange is part author (with Noboru Kawazoe) of a handsome new book (1962) on the Ise shrine (page 113), with photographs of great beauty by Yoshio Watanabe. He also wrote the text of a book on the Katsura Palace, Kyoto, illustrated by Yasuhiro Ishimoto's photographs (Yale University Press, 1960).

Hiroshi Oe, b. 1913

Specializes in school and university buildings. Besides being a practising architect he is professor at Hosei University, Tokyo, for whom he designed, in 1953 (completed 1958), an important group of buildings in reinforced concrete, one of the few buildings of architectural note put up by the many universities in Tokyo (page 153). He graduated from Tokyo University, and his other buildings include houses, an office block (the Miki Building) in Tokyo and several schools, most notably his two Toyoeiwa-Sogakuin schools.

Takamasa Yoshizaka, b. 1917

Professor at Waseda University and a writer (his books include one on Le Corbusier and a translation of *Le Modulor*) as well as a practising architect. After a childhood spent in Europe (his father was a diplomat), he studied architecture at Waseda and stayed on there as a research graduate. In 1950 he went to Paris and spent three years in Le Corbusier's office. Since his return to Japan he has built houses in Tokyo and Kobe, the Japanese pavilion

Above: cultural centre, Nichinan (1962). Facing page: Kagawa prefectural offices, Takamatsu (1958). Both buildings by Kenzo Tange.

for the Venice *biennale*, 1956, lecture-rooms for Meisei University, Osaka, 1958, a teaching block for Kaisei University, Nagasaki, 1959, and a town-hall at Gotsu, 1962 (page 58). He was one of the three Japanese architects (Maekawa and Sakakura being the others) who acted as executive architects for Le Corbusier's Museum of Western Art in Ueno Park, Tokyo, 1959 (page 29).

Yoshinobu Ashihara, b. 1918

Graduated at Tokyo University and, after the war, entered Sakakura's office. In 1949 he set up on his own and designed a health centre at Yawata. In 1952 he went to America on a Fulbright scholarship, first to Yale and then to Harvard. After taking his Master's degree at Harvard he worked with Marcel Breuer. He returned to Japan in 1954 and has designed a number of houses, an office building (the Chuon-Koron building) in Tokyo, a women's hostel in Yokohama, an industrial club at Matsukama, the municipal hospital at Yokohama, 1959 (page 140), a youth hostel at Nikko, 1959, the Nikko hotel in the centre of Tokyo, 1961, and a cultural centre at Yatsushiro, 1962. He is now working on a gymnastics hall at Komazawa Park, Tokyo, which (together with Murata's athletics stadium) will form part of the secondary arena of the 1964 Olympic games.

Motowo Take, b. 1919

Studied at Waseda University, Tokyo,

where he is now a professor of city planning. Worked in Shanghai before the war. Author of a book on theatre and cinema architecture. His buildings

Above: exterior and interior of a house in Tokyo (Villa Coucou) by Takamasa Yoshizaka, 1957.

Left: Nagasaki City Hall by Motowo Take.

Below: youth hostel at Nikko, showing the entrance and the west side, by Yoshinobu Ashihara, 1959.

Right: Kiyonori Kikutake.
Below: a house in Tokyo by
Yoshinobu Ashihara.

show, more than most of the modern Japanese architects, the influence of Frank Lloyd Wright as well as that of Le Corbusier. His principal buildings are: sports hall and community centre, Sendai, 1952; school at Michiru, 1955; aquarium at Nagasaki (his birthplace), 1959—a building in which a reinforced concrete frame is combined with local stone; additions in 1962 made it one of the best equipped aquaria in the world; city hall, Nagasaki, 1962.

Masato Otaka, b. 1923

A member of the five-man 'Metabolism' group—see under Kiyonori Kikutake below and on pages 146 and 155—whose town-planning studies are an important lead into the future. He was at Tokyo University and then in Maekawa's office, where he played a large part in the design of the concert-hall and library at Yokohama (pages 47 and 141), the cultural centre at Fukushima and the Harumi housing project (page 147). He has only recently set up practice on his own.

Kiyonori Kikutake, b. 1928

One of the most notable of the younger generation of architects which is following the lead of the small group—

Maekawa, Tange, Sakakura—which established modern architecture in Japan as the West now knows and admires it. He and a group of young architects, some of whom had been fellow students with him at Waseda University under Professor Motowo Take (who brought Waseda during the 1950s to rival Tokyo University as the main nursery of advanced architectural ideas), undertook a number of research and town-planning projects, and published some of them under the collective imprint of the 'Metabolism' group—see pages 146, 155 and 156. They constitute some of the most promising evidence of the younger Japanese architects' interest in social and town-planning ideas.

On leaving Waseda University Kikutake worked for a short time with the Takenaka contracting firm and with Murano and Mori in Osaka, but in 1953 he started on his own. He has built houses and flats (including a house for himself, 1958), a gymnasium for the Hitotsubashi secondary school in Tokyo (page 155), and the Shimane prefectural museum and art gallery at Matsue, 1960 (page 65)—see also page 61 for his treasury building under construction at Izumo Grand Shrine.

Fumihiko Maki, b. 1928

Another of the group of young architects (see under Kikutake and Otaka) who have pioneered modern town-planning and similar research under Tange's tutelage, and a member of the 'Metabolism' group (see pages 146 and 155). Maki has the most international experience of the young Japanese architects. After graduating from Tokyo University, he took a Master's degree at Cranbrook Academy, USA, and went on from there to Harvard. He worked afterwards in the offices of Skidmore, Owings and Merrill, José Luis Sert and, back in Japan, Kenzo Tange. He

Exterior and interior of a house in Tokyo (for his own occupation) by Kiyonori Kikutake, 1958.

has been responsible for one important building in Japan: the Toyoda auditorium at Nagoya University (page 123), the commission for which was first given to the Takenaka contracting firm and passed by them to Maki, who has a family connection with the firm. Maki is now in America, serving as an assistant professor at Washington University.

In 1961 he published (in conjunction with the Takenaka contracting company) an unusually far-sighted redevelopment plan for the Dojima area of Osaka, just across the river from the main business centre, in which he introduced the idea of the pedestrian precinct and the super-block containing communal services.

An example of modern Japanese industrial architecture: iron foundry at Saitama, Tokyo, by Naibu Akashi—see page 157. Above: a general view. Right: a close-up at one end, showing the external steel frame.

PHOTOGRAPHERS

J. M. Richards: pages 14, 21, 23, 24, 25 (bottom), 28 (top right), 41, 43, 45, 46, 47 (two bottom), 49, 54, 55, 57, 58 (top right), 59, 62, 64, 65, 68 (centre and bottom), 69, 71, 72, 74, 75, 76, 77, 79 (bottom), 80, 84, 85, 86, 87, 88 (top), 93, 95, 97 (bottom), 100, 101, 103 (bottom), 104 (bottom left), 112, 113, 115, 116, 120, 125 (bottom), 127, 131, 136 (top), 139, 141 (top), 148 (bottom).

Shikenchiku: page 22.

Akio Kawasumi: pages 25 (top), 26, 28 (excepting top right), 32, 34, 35, 36, 123, 124, 125 (centre and top), 126, 138, 149, 150, 151, 153 (top), 181, 184.

Chuji Hirayama: pages 29, 30 (top), 142, 176 (two bottom), 178 (top), 179 (top), 182 (two top).

Kiyoshi Otsuji: pages 27, 33.

Yoshio Watanabe: pages 30 (bottom), 31 (bottom), 51, 172 (bottom), 173.

S. Shigihara: pages 52, 108 (top), 111.

Toshio Taira: pages 58 (top left and bottom), 66, 67, 68 (top), 78, 79 (top), 83, 97 (top), 98, 103 (top), 104 (top and bottom right), 106, 107, 108 (bottom), 109 (top), 135 (bottom), 176 (two top), 179 (bottom), 180.

R. T. Paine: page 61 (top).

Takenaka Co.: page 104 (two centre).

Shokokusha: page 105.

Kiyoo Kanayama: pages 119, 121, 122, 141 (bottom), 175 (centre and bottom right).

Yukio Futagawa: pages 132, 133, 134, 137 (top), 145 (bottom), 147, 148 (top), 153 (bottom).

Fumio Murasawa: pages 140, 152.

Aso: page 154.

Bunji Kobayashi: page 159.

Kokusai Kenchiku: page 174.

Bauen & Wohnen, Zurich: pages 175 (bottom left), 177, 178 (bottom), 182 (bottom).

O. Murai: page 185.

In addition to the photographers listed above, and to the Japanese magazine *Shinkenchiku*, whose help over both photographs and plans is acknowledged on page 8, thanks are due to the Swiss magazine *Bauen & Wohnen* for information about the plans of some of the buildings illustrated and to Professor Kobayashi from whose book, *Japanese Architecture*, the two drawings on page 94 are taken.

INDEX